SPIRITUAL SCIENCE

SPIRITUAL SCIENCE

MAGAZINE SPRING 2014

CONTENTS

SPIRITUAL SCIENCE

Volume 1, Number 1

PUBLISHER

Infinite Elevation Publishing
Natalie Jean

GRAPHIC DESIGNER

Erline Germain

BUSINESS OFFICE

11115 Lund Place
Kensington, MD 20895

Graphics courtesy
Getty Images & Stock
Xchange. All rights
reserved to those
agencies.

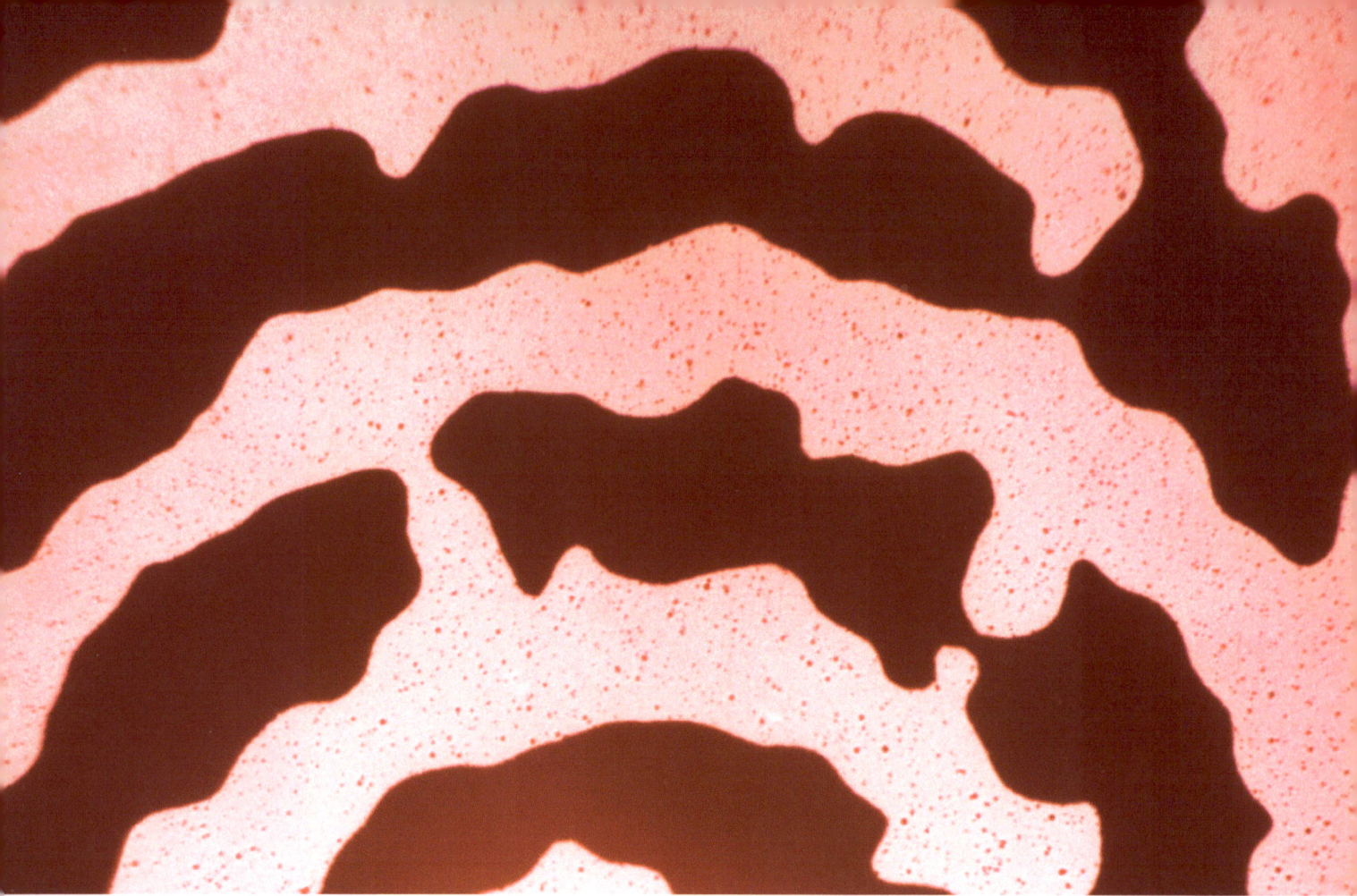

My Truth Revealed

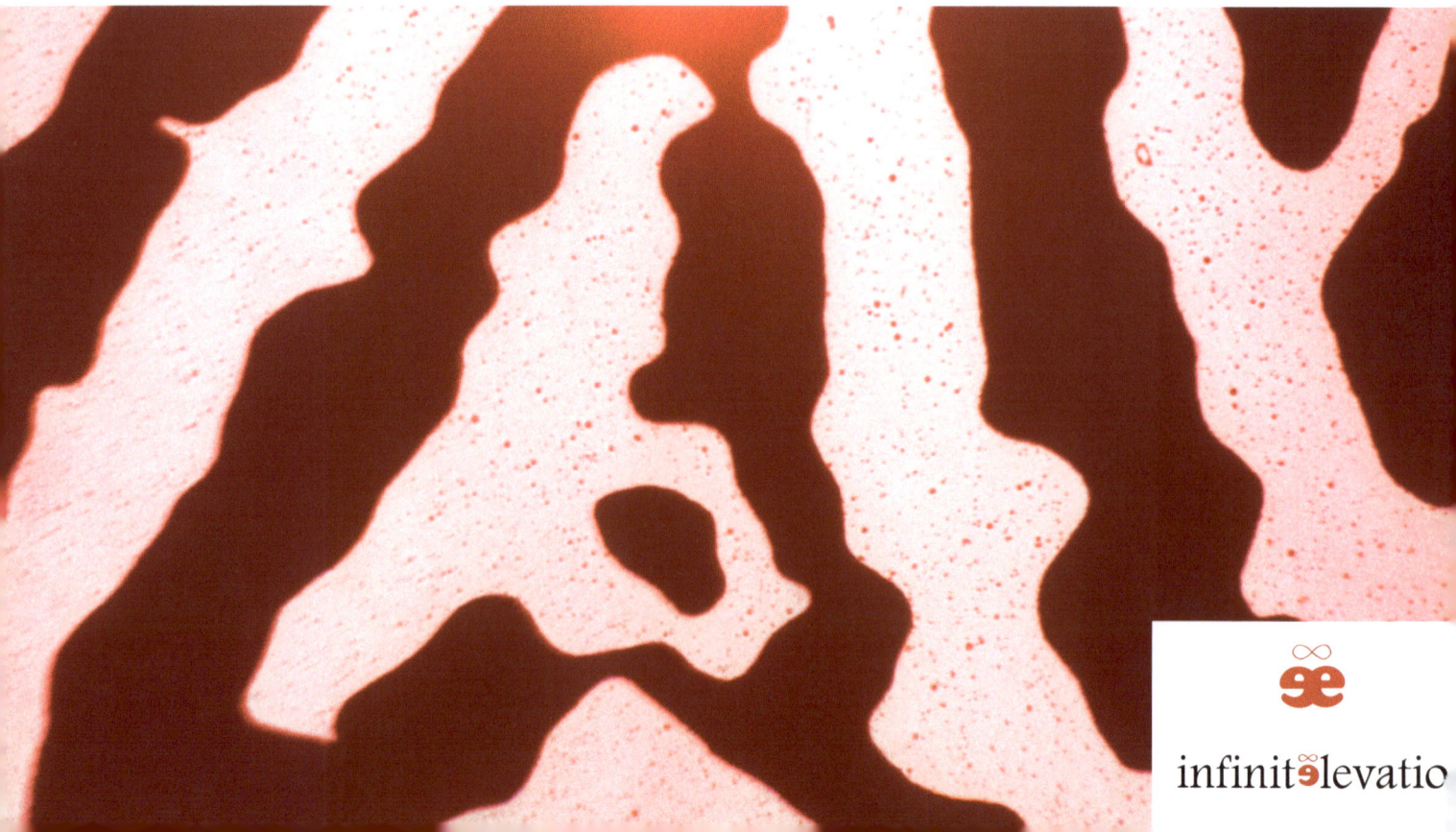

infinit elevatio

Greetings

It seems that the Scientists of the country need a publication which will represent their work satisfactorily.

Mrs. Ida A. Nichols has responded to the need, which the promise of a magazine which shall state things essential concerning the science and be without reproach of whim, caprice, or falsifying.

It is promised that the advertising rates shall be within reach of even the poorest of us.

A very judicious mode of handling written contributions will prove to many workers in the Science - field how much undeveloped talent there is among them and it is hoped that everybody practicing or teaching Science will try their hand at writing for this monthly.

For my own part I am most pleased with the purpose and underlying spirit which prompt the issuing of this little publication, and therefore for the present I have withdrawn from writing for the ably conducted older periodicals to help set this young candidate for favor quite on its feet.

Talks before the Association, reports of Sermons, Bible Lessons, answers to questions, and many a little paragraph will be written by myself to you, reader, every month, for the purpose of :

1st. Helping you into further light upon Christian Science.
2nd. Healing you of your sickness, pain, and unhappiness.
3rd. Awakening an interest in the practical workings of the Science.
4th. Urging you to work.
5th. Urging you to subscribe to the magazine.

Ida
Ida A. Nichols

I AM Excited to bring Spiritual Science Magazine out into the Universe. This magazine was originally called Christian Science Magazine in the late 1800's. It was created by Ida Nichols. Emma Curtis Hopkins wrote her International Bible lessons for the magazine, as well as having her Association meeting notes. About 4 years ago, I fell in love with Emma Curtis Hopkins and her teachings through my ministerial course, given by Dr. Rev. Christopher Bazemore, at the Church of the Holy Spirit Divine Science, in Largo MD. I was awed at the way they spoke about speaking your Truth and Identifying yourself with the power within, which is God. I was so moved by her teachings, I scoured the world for more. Upon my research, I had the privilege of meeting Rev. Joanna Rogers and Rev. Michael Terranova. Together, we found many of Emma's missing lessons, and are working diligently to make them available to the world. Rev. Terranova was able to find copies of the old Christian Science Magazines. My idea was to create an online magazine with the same material, while adding a new spin to the old version. This is a treasure!! For now, the magazine will be an online magazine. I am currently working on the publication where readers will be able to purchase a subscription. I hope that these articles will move you in the way that they have

Natalie
Natalie Jean

To *Love* Thyself *Is* To *Know* Thyself

Conceived from one thought, through the uniting of two souls, a wonderful beautiful Spirit is born. The only thing it knows is love. The only thing it understands is Love. Born with only love in mind, perfection is all that it can see, feel, and know. Trust in Truth. Goodness is infinite. It doesn't know anything else. Everything around it is good. This is its expectation. This is all that it knows. Its life is filled with joy and ease. Its only memories are of the One that gave it life. This wonderful Spirit is you and I.

From birth to earth, we begin to walk on the path of illusions.

As we grow older, our emotions seem to change. Love seems to not exist. The human conditioning seems to take over. This human conditioning is a veil of disbelief in the real, which makes us feel uneasy about who we are, undermines our self worth, torments our very nature. We are pulled in many different directions. Living by other peoples' rules, following someone else's dream. The pursuit of happiness, by someone else's concept. We gravitate towards the mundane, rather than towards that thing that would bring us back to life. Looking over our shoulders, we look at the successes of our friends, families, and co-workers. We begin to question our worthiness. Thoughts circle round and round in our mind, as we try to stay planted to the ground. Something tries to pull us down into an abyss of self-resistance. And yet there is a resistance not to let ourselves falter. We begin to question our purpose here in the Universe, wondering "Who AM I?" We will eventually learn that we are actually the reverse, " I AM."

It is interesting that we tend to ask the question of our existence because something has gone terribly wrong in our lives. We know that there is a better way and that life was not meant to be so difficult. To find this answer, we will do everything possible to get it in our midst.   On our quest, we tend to want to go to every bookstore possible to find the answer. We might even buy 10 books on the same subject, eager with anticipation that the answer will come to us. Workshops after workshops, the answer still has not come. We are seeking to be spiritually fed. Yet the answer has always been there. There are many religions out in the Universe, and anyone of them can give you the answer that you seek. But the only person standing in your way is you. Then the question really is, are you ready for the answer? Are you ready to receive all that it is you desire? We all want to know the answer to the great big puzzle, but at the same time we fear our own greatness. What happens when self-realization takes place? Where will we go from here? We need to be firm in what we want

and to know what to do when we get it.

When we are seeking to know our purpose in life, the real thing that we are seeking is to know what love really means. It is interesting how in the beginning of life, we know exactly who we are. But because of the external world, we become confused. The thinking becomes the real issue for us . Emma Curtis Hopkins, a new thought leader from the late 1800s says, "There is only stopping our thinking. The great vacuum of silence, is stillness, of ceasing from thoughts is suction for the strength and understanding of Spirit. He who stops thinking is greater than he who thinks the highest doctrines he has ever heard. He who does nothing is the greatest workers. He lets Spirit work." (From her book, Bible Interpretations Fourth Series). We forget what it means to let go and let Spirit. As children our focus is centered on love and joy. There is nothing else we need to know. It is almost as if we need to be childlike to

know Truth. The real answer to this big puzzle is there is a need to know love. We want some type of satisfaction in our life. In our society, it seems to love oneself, is the act of being conceited. But what it really means is that we love Spirit as we love ourselves.

Love is great. It is the greatest power in the Universe. But we must be able to know and speak the Truth about it. Our thoughts and words are our daily projections, whatever we see in front of us on a daily basis is that thing we have created through our mind and word. We can't seem to understand why things happen to us, we want to blame others and we consistently want to blame Spirit. But Spirit has nothing to do with this. We were born with free will. In fact we were born with the answer. We have chosen to allow this human veil to cover us, so that the truth Is not uncovered. You must be able to represent who you are in this life, by your own Truth. To speak the Truth of oneself is to show

forth to the world what you want in return. Speaking the Truth of yourself means to state that you are the essence of love.

The question now, is how do we get to a place of self love. There are eight wonderful concepts that you need to learn. These would include:

1. Knowing that you are worthy

2. Knowing that you are deserving

3. Loving Thyself and acceptance of love

4. Accepting all experiences as Good

5. Using Power of Forgiveness

6. Understanding that our lives were created by us

7. Knowing that there is Good for you

8. Using Self-Realization

Let us begin with worthiness. Many of us would like to manifest great blessings and miracles in our life, and no matter how hard we try nothing seems to happen. We never take the time to ask ourselves how we truly feel about ourselves. Do you believe that you are worthy enough to get the things you want out of life? At times, we tend to care about how others feel about us, rather than how we feel about ourselves. We need to come to understanding that Spirit never makes any mistakes and that

we are worthy of all the love. It is about how you feel about yourself, not what others think about you. A great way to see how you feel about yourself is to write down what you feel are your best attributes and your worst attributes. If there are things that you don't like, then you definitely don't think that you are worthy of anything. Using positive affirmations to heal that idea will change those concepts. But you must not just say the words, you must be able to embody them as well.

Second, you must know that you are deserving of all. A lot of times people will question why some deserve some things and others do not. This is not even the point, it doesn't matter what other people have, what matters is that you know that you deserve everything that you want, just by the fact that you were born from Spirit. Everyone deserves the ultimate amount of success in their life. You don't have to be the greatest scientist or anything else. You need to be you, a person full of harmony, peace, and joy. Someone who seeks out his/her passions and does everything from the heart. The misconception is that there are some that are chosen. The Truth is that we are all chosen for some great purpose.

Third, love thyself and accept love in return. In order for you

to gain anything in life, you need to love yourself and know that everything about you is great. You must also accept that someone else can love you as well. Often times, love will come to those who love themselves because this is what they are projecting out to the world. How we feel about ourselves is how others will treat us. This is why some people in abusive relationships fail to leave because they often have low self-esteem, and believe that they were meant to be treated in such a fashion. A great way to get to love yourself is to wake up every morning and say positive affirmations about yourself. You can say "I Am beautiful," I Am made from His perfection." "I love everything about me, I have a great purpose."

Fourth, accepting all experiences as Good. We all go through challenges in our lives. At the end of the challenges, there is something that we have learned. It allows us to take another step towards life. Many find this concept hard, especially when some have gone through horrendous challenges. We survived them and we must forge ahead, knowing that these experiences bring us closer to our Oneness with Spirit. They teach us not to repeat the same pattern, and that there are better ways of living.

Fifth, power of forgiveness. One of the hardest concepts for most people. We allow the past to fester within our systems for so long that it can make us sick and restless. This is no way to live. The other people who have offended you in some way are living their lives happily, while you mourn the past. You must learn to let it go. You must learn to wish the best for all and to know nothing will ever harm us again. Emma Curtis Hopkins suggests that we keep this understanding, "There is nothing to hurt us, rob us, or defile us. "Greet all things as Spirit." (Bible Interpretations Fourth Series).

Sixth, we create our life. Emma Curtis Hopkins (Bible Interpretations Fourth Series) says that "It is what we think within our hearts independent of our speech and independent of our true Spirit, which determines our destiny." This is so true. However, we often want to blame others, especially Spirit for everything that has gone wrong in our lives. It is time for us to take responsibility for what we have projected with our thoughts, words, and hearts. Imagine if the world were to only think and use positive words, what type of world we would have today? Your words and thoughts can destroy or they can create life. So, if there is something that you want out of life, you need to stay positive and know that all is well. You also need to know that things are happening in the Now!! So many times others want to tell us how to live our lives, and we listen to the noise, creating even more havoc in our lives. It is about tuning into our own belief systems. A good way to work on this is to take ten minutes a day to meditate and sit in the silence. Listen to the voice within, guiding you to your next step.

Seventh, knowing there is Good for you and you ought to have it. There is a world of Good out there in the Universe and it belongs to everyone. If you want the Goodness to be in your life, you have to believe that it is out there for you and everyone. Also, you must remember that the Good you want already resides within you. Spirit is the power within you. No one can take that away from you. It is waiting for you to listen to its call, so that you can know how to use it.

Eighth, finally when all is understood, you will come to the final conclusion of Self-Realization. You will come to your own understanding of your connection to Spirit. You will understand that you do not have to beg and plead for the perfect life. You just have to accept that it is already here for you. You must focus on the here an now. Not waiting for tomorrow to acquire what you need, but knowing it is already here now. Bringing the invisible to the visible.

Now, watch as this transformation takes place, many things will come to life. Friends and family that once supported you, will not understand this new found happiness. Then the real noise will begin. They will try to sway you to come back to their way of thinking. At this point, you will need to stand firm to your beliefs. New friends and those with the same understanding will come to your life. You will be the same person, but with a clearer understanding of a connection so grand. You will be renewed with a new sense of purpose. No one will have the power to move you, but you will have the power to move mountains. You go back to the beginning, like a child, knowing all is well and that you are completely loved and supported by the Universe.

Once you find the answer, your life begins to change dramatically. Friends and family that once supported you, won't understand you. Then the noise begins. What is this noise you ask, it is the noise of everyone around you telling you that what you are doing is wrong. You will find new friends with a new understanding. There is a consequence of your own understanding and happiness.

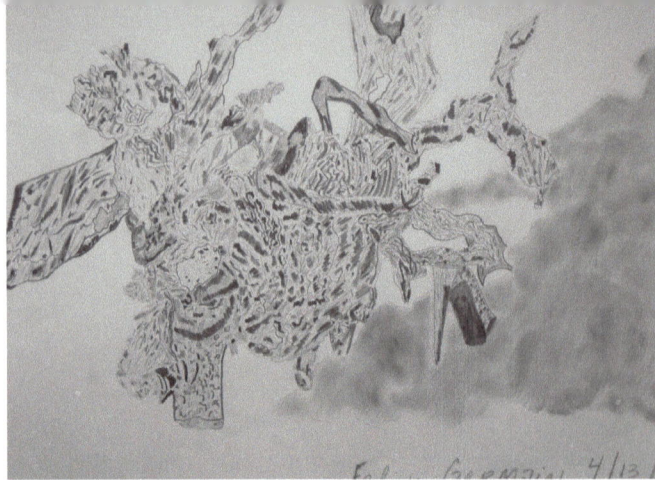

CREATIVE INSPIRATION

It comes in all shapes and forms. My creativity has been with me for so long. Whether I acknowledged it or not, is the question. To be raised with a stellar education and dump it in the world of freedom is a taboo. I am an artist. I am unafraid to say it. I have learned to tame the creative energies. They will flair up if you do not tend to them. It is a real situation. A real life shaping thing to do. Sometimes this takes a great deal of time to come to understand. But it is a truth we must face about ourselves. I have been on this journey for so long it seems and I still feel I have not tapped into the entire breath of me. Whenever I am led to this well, I will take it upon myself to fully appreciate and express gratitude for the blessings the Spirit has given me. If you'd like me to share a bit more feel free to email me at *germain.erline@gmail.com*. Just know that it is within you to create and be whatever it is you dream to be. Be fearless and brave.

-Erline Germain

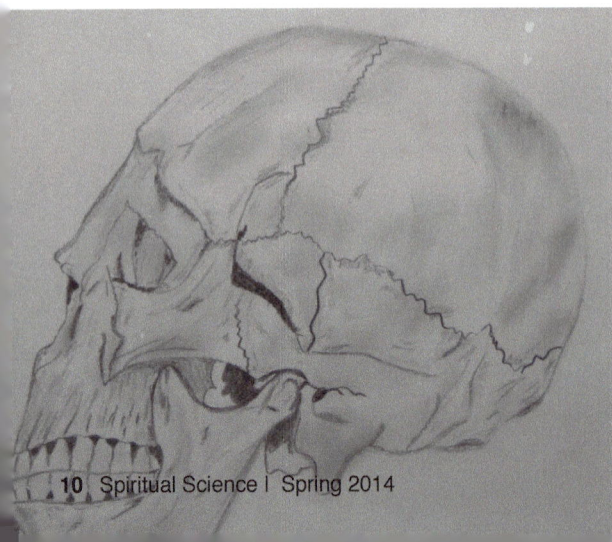

THEMES OF LIFE by Pervenia Brown

I believe one of the themes of life is to assist others. How you assist others is your lesson to learn. If you were born and brought up in an environment where distrust, mistrust, and ulterior motives exist, the residue of those themes may still exist today, playing out in various aspects of your life. The intensity of discomfort you feel within yourself is telling, and may reveal itself through the personal stories of others. If you are intrigued by personal stories of triumph, in awe of everyday people, who selflessly volunteer their time to help others struck by illness or crises, then you recognize these themes.

Personal stories are humbling and poignant. People who personify this level of compassion embody fortitude, tenacity, and love—everything a companion or caring person typifies. If that part of your psyche was injured at an early age, it has to heal. Ask yourself: "When was the last time I genuinely helped someone without expecting something in return?" Can you hear your ego defending itself? "[C]onflicts with inner guidance in which you are drawn to reach out to another and yet are uncertain about offering help . . . do not reflect poorly on you. Instead, they indicate that you have potential goodness that has yet to be expressed. Your ego often views what it is asked to give as 'unreasonable,' because the ego measures what it gives so carefully. But the ego fears empowering another person and therein lies the root of the human conflict: do I empower you when I intuitively sense that I can or do I withhold this gift because I fear you may become more than me?"

Are you aware that motives can shroud pure intentions? Do voices in your head warn incessantly against being taken advantage of? Should you ignore your inner voice of reason and jump to assist everyone in need that crosses your path? Distinctions must be made. "Discriminating judgments are essential to making choices in the world, but let the mind be guided by reason, not bound by it." Nonetheless, we admire altruism in others. I suppose that's the balance in life.

While unsupportive environments can contaminate pure intentions, it is the Spirit within which we assist others that reveal our true intentions. What is the theme of your life? Knowing that ulterior motives can ruin wholesome intentions, let go mentally of the cumulative weight of distrust, mistrust and ulterior motives and feel liberated. Feel your energy flow freely. Follow inner guidance and cultivate healthy intentions.

Edenic Cherubim

There are bright words in literature which charm with mysterious beauty. They rivet thought. They halo truth. Such rendez-vous for the hearts and minds of men contain germs of pure wisdom. They are familiar with the forevers. Such is the word Eden or Happiness. Such is Cherubim, whch means perfect knowledge.

The symbols of Truth woo and win us to Revelation. Look through them at the Spirit and rejoice. We know astronomy through the telescope. We enter Eden through the Cherubim, that is, we become happy by the perfect knowledge. Perfect knowledge is Truth, which is Christ. So that we see that we are saved through Christ.

Perfect knowledge is "eternal life" according to Jesus. So we understand why the Cherubim "keep the way of the tree of life." Christ says "I am the Way, the Truth and the Life." Here is a gospel promise instead of a divine punishment.

All that keeps men from perfect knowledge or Edenic Happiness is ignorance. So blame not God that you do not own a villa on the river Gihon. Send home the responsibility and know that ignorance is your calamity, your exile; that you are your own Devil.

Men are inclined to make Cerberi out of the Cherubim. They do not guard Eden like "dogs in the manger," but are living witnesses, calling us to enter and become "heirs of eternal life." Angels delight in the salvation of men, (1 Pet. 1:12), and the Cherubim are no exception.

It would have been sad indeed if God had not made a door in the wall which ignorance built about the garden of Eden. These Cherubim were at the east-gate, the sun-rising-gate, the Resurrection; they are the gate. So Christ says, "I am the door;" "I am the Resurrection." We shall enter Eden, awaken in His likeness at the rising of the sun of righteousness, with healing in his wings.

Notice that there were two Cherubim manifest the fatherhood and motherhood of God. The Holy Spirit or Mother principle of the Deity is just taking hold of the world in this age of women. It is sublimely and infinitely significant that our civilization is beginning to emphasize the power and purity of motherhood in the science of life. This renewing influence of the Spirit of Love is to be demonstrated by a "new Heaven and a new earth." This is the ruling Spirit of the Millennium.

"September suns are smiling
In the earth's uplifted face.
And far and near
The woods and hills
and skies embrace."

What Will Revive Us?

What a wonder there is going up all over the lands, why there has never been a time since the days of the Apostles when the look of a Christian would heal of palsy; the word of a Christian bring clean strong flesh for leprous scales; the preaching of a Christian turn public wrongs into efforts to bless the poor.

Earnest preachers have besought the Lord for a Pentecostal outpouring such blessed simple-hearted Peter of Galilee, when with one sermon he added to the church 3000 new names. But no such outpouring has been vouchsafed. Why?

Because nobody has preached pure Christian doctrine. Has anybody ever told us from the pulpit or preacher's stand that the Truth shall make us free? Has anybody shown what freedom consists in? Has any body told us that no bonds are possible to the Christian? The inefficiency in any direction, incapacity, foolishness, sickness, poverty, slavery, weariness, pain, are impossible when we really have heard the voice of Truth and rejoiced in her words?

Has anybody told us that if we really hear Truth we can actually be given the power to speak in foreign languages without a teacher, prophesy, of things to come, raise people off sick beds, stop death's work, speak with tongues of fire to rouse men and women from despair and open prison houses with keys? No? Then nobody has preached Christian doctrine-alas for the terrified world!

But when Peter and the eleven were freshly from Christ's plainly worded teachings they preached it with just these unfailing results.

He had ascended out of their sight to carry on his work in the invisible kingdom and given directions that they should wait for an expect the power of the Holy Ghost or full power of Truth to take effect upon them, after which they could speak with boldness and certainty of those things he had taught them. They believed in this and were waiting together in a certain place.

Suddenly a sound from heaven as of a rushing mighty wind came and the house was filled with its shivering.

Then they saw the signs of a vivific Intelligence intended for each of them.

Signs, signs, signs of power in the old days were given to all who heard Truth and preached and taught and practiced it. Not only was the word there but the outward sign of it wherever the mind was so constituted that it needed some visible token of the nearness of the Presence that demanded such mysterious performances.

They were at Jerusalem, in the year of our Lord 33, on the day of the Pentecost, a thanksgiving feast day of the Jews.

The Apostles without fear of men or evil happenings opened their lips and spake as they had been taught, of the divine character and awful majesty of the man, whom the council of Priests and elders had taken and by wicked hands crucified and slain.

As they spake of his rising from the grave and ascending up on high to judge the world in righteousness, their listeners were pricked to the heart and cried out in terror-

"Men and brethren what shall we do?"

To this the apostles had but one answer, the same that is given to-day to the same question:

"Repent and be baptized."

But notice, the nature of the preaching had been such as to make them willingly, easily repent.

According to the demands of the present interpretation it is a difficult thing to repent. Yet to the end of the world it was promised that right preaching should make people gladly repent.

No one disputes that it must have been Truth that these imbued and inspired men preached.

It saved the people who heard it from sin and sickness and poverty.

The restless world is asking what is the Truth whose preaching will save like this? And Science, which answers all things, but whose light has been haughtily refused by Scripture teachers in all the past,

answers by just one statement: There is but one God. This preaching will take the citadels of wickedness and fire the simplest mind with fervid keenness.

It will pour out upon the sons and daughters of men a baptism of prophecy and thrilling spiritual wisdom to do miracles of healing and helping.

There is but one Force and Law Giver; there is but one Deity-one God, and we his children the work of his hands, his likeness and image, all the work of but One Mind, and that a perfect mind incapable of making any imperfect thing; incapable of mistake or error.

But a belief in another Deity, another Force and Law Giver, has hidden the true from our faces.

Let us repent of our sin or error and be baptized with the fill moving of the power of Truth which turning from such error will lead us into,

He will preach earnestly of this One Power only, who will mix his word with no hint of any other force in all the universe but this, will stir the nations to repentance, will lift the awful yoke of that other power which pulpit, press, missionaries and philanthropist have laid upon us.

He will cause the islands of the sea to laugh, and the lands that knew no joy to sing with gladness.

The pulpit everywhere has given name and place to a great Force and Law Giver who is not Good.

The press has given the children of men over into the clutches of this awful force.

Missionaries wail and lament that so few can be found to rescue the people of the world from such clutches.

And philanthropists keep statistics and records of the workings of this Force through men and women and children, and even inanimate matter and animal life.

The name of this awful Force is Evil. Everywhere people believe

in its power. All the blessed Truth that preachers tell is mixed by falsehoods about the doings and dealings of this great power.

What wonder that Truth, the stirring, reviving, moving power, will not consent to thrill with the winds of her presence idolators,--those who do not sever her with all the heart by speaking only of One Force and One Presence!

Only this Truth will revive the Apostolic days of power. Only this preaching will gladden the multitudes. When one can be found to speak of the wonder and mightiness that people who hear this will enjoy, none will return to the service of the old Powers.

And to the number of such as are saved each church many add her countless followers. Now and then a voice is being lifted protesting against old beliefs, but it carries not the old potency because none yet speaking have risen completely out of the old beliefs and old terrors; ambitions and petty strifes are still believed to be necessary to help on the speakers and teachers of the law.

But we see these follies dying out as Truth forces the young followers of the new doctrine into purer and purer thoughts and life.

And out from the ranks of even these there shall arise apostles to speak with tongues of fire; a Peter to rouse a multitude, and many who shall with the true word revive and ignorance and move to repentance and righteousness all the world that has served another deity.

These shall cry aloud, Awake, oh world that sleepiest in false beliefs! Awake to righteousness and sin not! And the sleeping world will turn from her idolatry. Then there shall be no more pain, neither sorrow nor crying.

TWO ITEMS

by Mrs. L.A. Gooding

I have had some strange and lovely experiences since entering upon the study and practice of Christian Science. Some of the workers have asked me to write up two of them so I will do so.

One day a lady with an ugly tumor on her eye called to see me for treatment. The tumor seemed a very real condition to me, very far indeed from the unreality I had been taught that such things are. But I faithfully committed the whole matter into the hands of "the Father," and treated her in Science. Two days after she called again. "How do you do to-day?" I asked, of course thinking first and foremost of the eye I had treated, and secretly hoping, as all young Scientists do, that she would tell me she was getting better. "Look and see for yourself," she said smilingly. I looked, the green shade was taken off-the tumor had completely disappeared. "Is it possible!" I exclaimed. "What did you do for it?" She was more astonished at my unscientific exclamation than I was. "Didn't you expect it would go?" she asked innocently. I came to my judgment with a jump. "O, yes, of course," I replied, straightening up with dignity.

Since I am not so off guard when people tell me they are cured of their maladies by Christian Science.

The second experience which I will now relate, the rest of you may put your own construction upon and explain your own way. All I can say is that it really happened to me while I was wide awake and in not the least uncanny mood of mind:

One evening I sat waiting as usual for my husband to come home from his business. I was thinking of nothing in particular but rocking and waiting as I so often do after the days work is done. Suddenly I seemed to see two great doors roll apart and leave exposed to my astonished gaze a fine country field with winding streams and white paths leading to a wonderful city beyond. Right ahead of me I saw my husband's grandmother, walking upright and strong with lithe as a young girl, every moment easy and graceful. As I knew that she was a poor rheumatic, with every limb out of shape and every joint stiff and swollen, of course I was more than interested. Coming toward her was my husband's mother, whose face was radiant with the light of something besides simple pleasure at greeting her with a light I was unfamiliar with.

"When did you come?" she asked of her, "I but just came," was the reply. "Did you have a hard time coming over?" "No, I just closed my eyes and the first thing I knew I was here." They seemed to move forward together. Then I saw her grandson, who long since left this earth, coming joyously forward. He greeted his grandmother tenderly. "When did you come, dear?" "Did you have a hard time coming over?" "Not at all, I just closed my eyes and the first thing I knew I was here." "Oh! there is Oliver!" and grandmother sprang forward with rapturous joy to greet her son who had been passed from earth many a long year. After the greeting he asked the same questions exactly which the others had asked, "When did you come?" 'I just came." Did you have a hard time coming over?" "No, I closed my eyes and the first thing I knew I was here."

The great doors suddenly closed. I heard my husband's footsteps. "Take me close to you," cried, trembling with a vague terror. "Hold me till I am not afraid. I have just seen grandma, and your mother and Bertie and Oliver. Grandma seemed to be entirely cured of her rheumatism. She walked lightly and as if she were happy and well instead of sick and suffering as we know she is." Without saying a word my husband took from his pocket a telegram he had just received, informing him of his grandmother's death the night before.

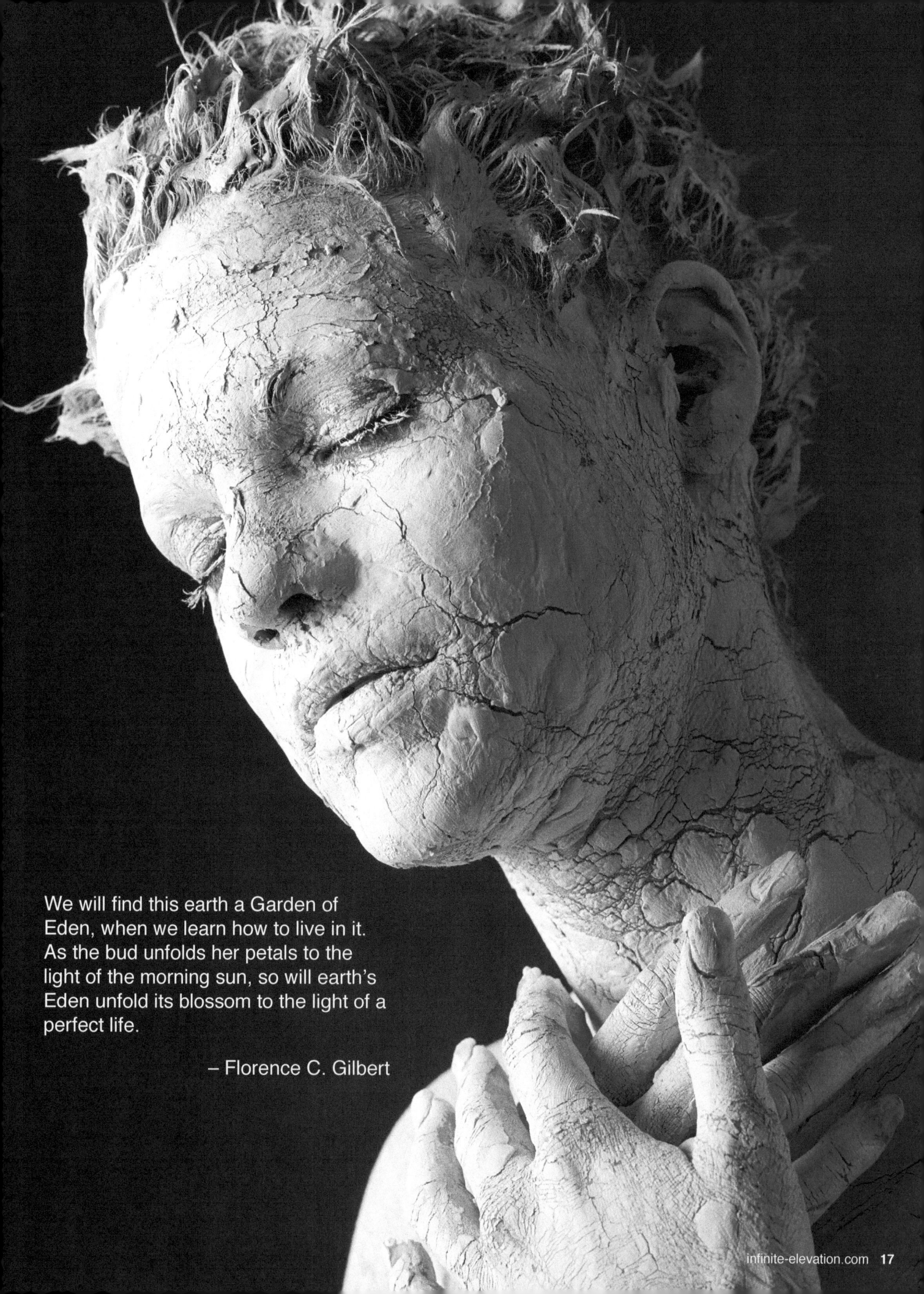

We will find this earth a Garden of Eden, when we learn how to live in it. As the bud unfolds her petals to the light of the morning sun, so will earth's Eden unfold its blossom to the light of a perfect life.

– Florence C. Gilbert

Infinitus Amour

The New Fragrance

from Infinite Elevation.

Love Infinitely

Order yours today!

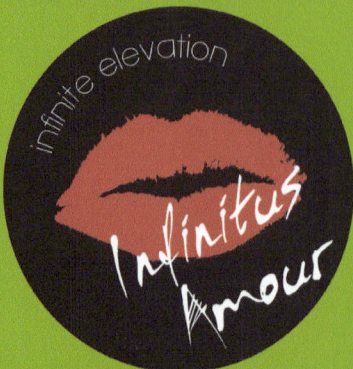

Manifestation of Self

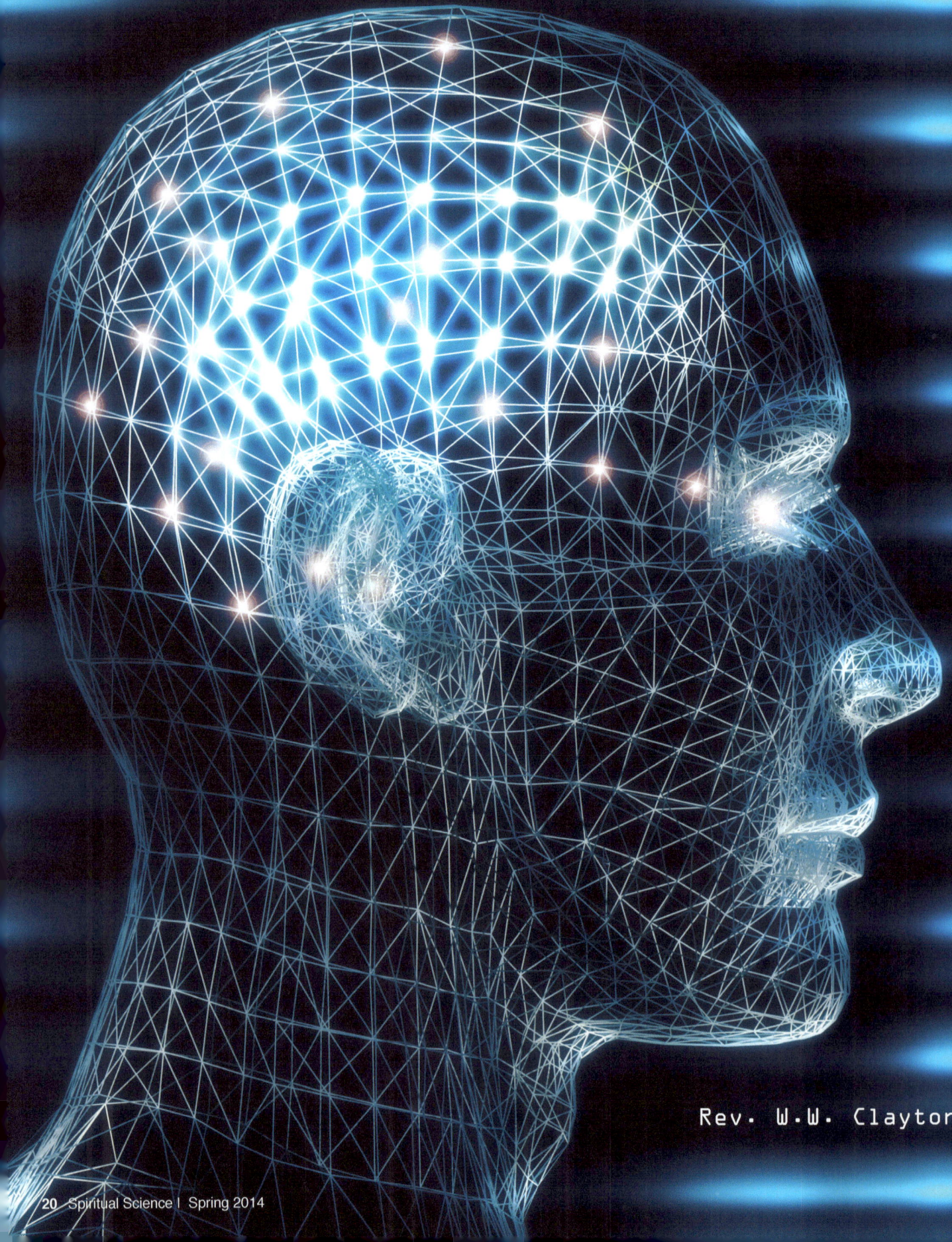

Rev. W.W. Clayton

Christian Science does not, like the story of Dr. Jekyll and Mr. Hyde, find it necessary to resort to the potency of a drug to explain the contradiction which appears in the characters of people. The doctrine of the false self-the mortal mind with its out showing-is a scientific explanation of the phenomenon.

The question is often asked us as Christian Scientists: "What progress is there for man if he is created perfect in the image of God?" We answer: Man's progress is that of manifestation, or the out showing of the perfect self.

Nature is not wanting in examples on the lower plane of vegetable life of what is known as pre-for-mation, or the existence of the perfect plant before the process of unfolding through germination and growth begins. It may be true that all forms are thus created in the Spirit or Thought of God, and that, after all, growth is not the building up of plant or animal from material accretions, but only its showing forth from a pre-existent perfect state. At all events, this may serve as an analogy of man, whom we have the best of reasons for believing is a pre-existent spirit or thought of God, and co-eternal with the Infinite Mind.

Somehow the thought is deep in our literature that the visible man is not the real man. Emerson says: "The eating, drinking, planting and calculating man does not represent man, but misrepresents him." Occasionally there has appeared on the earth a much superior being to the ordinary mortal, and undoubtedly a better representative of the true self. This has kept alive in man the natural intuition of his better self and has enabled poets, idealists and prophets to portray the glories of the coming man.

Occasionally in the same persons there are temporary flashes of higher qualities, showing that the true man is not far away from the false and seeming man.

The true man is the creation of God. "And God created man in His own image." The false and seeming man in His own image." The false and seeming man is the creation of mortal mind. "The carnal mind is enmity against God; it is not subject unto the law of God, neither indeed can be."

Paul brings out this quality and its conflict-the mortal mind and the spiritual mind-in his letter to the Romans, 7:19-24; "For the good that I would I do not, but the evil that would not that I do. Now if I do that I would not, it is no more I (the true self) that do it, but sin (mortal sin) that dwelleth in me....For I delight in the law of God after the inward man; but I see another law in my member warring against the law of my mind."

The true self is called by the apostle Peter "the hidden man of the heart," and "that which is incorruptible;" 1 Peter 3:4. This is the immortal man, hidden away for the present in vast multitudes, but which is to be revealed or made manifest in all.

We say man is the thought of God. This divine thought being the deepest in man is the seed, so to speak, which will ultimately realize its full fruition in perfect manifestation. This divine thought stirring in the creature causes that universal expectation of which Paul speaks when he says: "The earnest expectation of the creature waiteth for the manifestation of the sons of God." Romans 8:19. The word "creature" here means the whole rational creation, the species, ,an, and it is as if the apostle had said, "The whole human race carries in its bosom the instinct of its childship to the Father Spirit, and is only waiting to have that divine childship revealed or shown forth."

The true self is sonship with God. One son of God has been fully manifested, even Jesus Christ. But He is a sample of what all shall be. "For as we have borne the image of the earthy, we shall also bear the image of the heavenly."

But is not this to be beyond the grave? No, not necessarily. Says the apostle John: "Beloved, now are we the sons of God, and it doth not yet appear what we shall be." According to this the "manifestation of the sons of God" for which the whole creation is waiting, may be attained here in this world through truth which maketh free. Now we are the sons of God; now we attain to true self. The truth therefore shows out the real Man, or reveals the unmanifested childship of every human being.

The Apostle John not only declares that we are now the sons of God through the truth, but there are the measureless strides for us still to take towards the perfect manifestation of our being. "It doth not yet appear what we shall be; but we know that when He shall appear (in us) we shall be like Him." Christ manifested the true man and the disciples say, "We beheld His glory, as He appeared like an only begotten Son of the Father, full of grace and truth." So the same Christ or true self in us is the hope of our glory.

In the false self called mortal mind, man is an imperfect, sinful, diseased and dying creature. Mortal Mind, with its effigy, the mortal body, is the creation of man through error and false belief.

It is the office of the Christian Science to abolish and destroy mortal mind and to bring out the true Self of every man and woman.

Christian Science does this by denying away the error-mind and its outshowing of sin, sickness, and mortality, and invoking the good and true mind. In lodging the truth in the mind, or effecting a cure, we declare all sickness, sin, and death to be unreal and the good to be the only reality. The evil or disease (which is only false belief) proves its nothingness by disappearing. The good proves its reality and permanence by coming forth as the true Self, and assuming the rightful dominion which God conferred upon it in the beginning.

I append the following lines which occured to me among my earlier reflections upon this subject:

Man's true being is not built but shown. For he the perfect image is of God: Albeit hidden behind the clouds of sense, To manifest anew his light, as when The sun, full-orbed, has ceased to shine Upon the world, and in the darkness cast All things a changed, unnatural aspect wear, But when the obscuring veil is rent Shines forth in majesty, the King of Day; So man, the effulgent spark of Deity Light of the intellectual heavens, In clouds of error wrapped about, And in the thick darkness veiled Of mortal mind, shines not. Behind the clouds of Selfhood still abides In glory with the Soul of Light, Undimmed, again to shine resplendent,
When Truth's omnipotence shall rend the veil, And call it forth to light the world.

ORDER
YOUR COPY

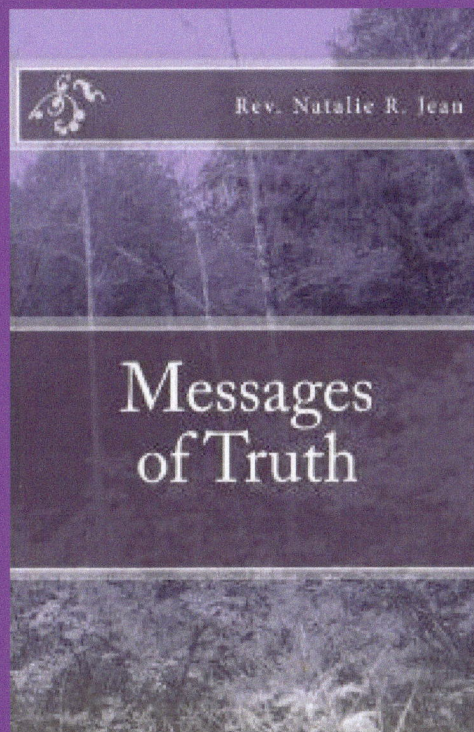

Rev. Natalie R. Jean

Messages of Truth

TODAY!

TEN VIRGINS

"And the door was shut."

This is one of the most difficult passages in the Bible and is very apt to be misunderstood. It is generally supposed to refer to a distant and arbitrary day of judgment when all further chance of reform or progress shall for ever be ended. This erroneous and cruel idea is an inheritance from the dark ages and can have no support in scientific religion.

"Write it in your heart that every day is the best day in the year. No man has learned anything rightly until he knows that every day is Doomsday."-Emerson.

It is unthinkable for God, who is Love, to ever cease loving. It would annihilate God's omnipresence. He is infinite love and unchangeable, and responds as readily to his children as the principle of mathematics responds to the mathematician. We cannot conceive of a time when Principle shall cease to be. We always "choose this day whom we will serve." As we journey on the broad way of the gratification of animal appetites, we close the door. As we discover that we are feeding on husks, and turn homeward, the Father is ready to receive us. It is not He who shuts the door, but his absence in the individual consciousness.

The results are not to be dreaded so much as that which leads to them. In other words, we need not hear the closed door, but that which closes it. The former is our friend and schoolmaster; the latter the tempter that kills the "life." Divine punishment, if punishment it must be called, is reformatory. God does not teach by corporal punishment but by Love alone. Love destroys the erroneous consciousness in the same way that Truth destroys the errors of students and awakens true and harmonious thought.

Wrong thinking closes the door, right thinking opens it and constitutes the way, the truth and the life; it leads to understanding of Creator and creature. "To know God" (to realize Truth) 'and Jesus the Christ," (to manifest the sonship), "is eternal life."

Character will be the "Shibboleth" demanded, and will itself determine, whether the door be open or closed.

My Love Ink!

Don't Become Discouraged

A.D.T. Whitney.

Don't be discouraged because you have a small number of patients. People are very slow to receive any new development of truth. You will often be met with the assertion, "if you cure this case, I will believe; your reputation will be made," or some such remark. They seem to say it in sincerity. But you cure the patient and it is passed over as lightly as you can imagine.

They will say it was the effect of past remedies, or there was probably not so much the matter as appeared to be, and often times those who have been your best friends in the past will shun you as an object to be feared.

Neither be discouraged because your patients seem ungrateful. This is too often the case, and especially by those who are treated free, although there are some grand exceptions. As we are not working for self-glory, we can let ingratitude pass. A true Christian healer cannot be discouraged by any of these experiences, which they all meet more or less, for their work is simply to do the will of God to the best of their understanding, and trust the conscequences to Him. Neither should a metaphysician be discouraged if they sometimes are overcome with the surrounding mentality, and thus suffer physical discord. To be sure,

a metaphysician should understand avoiding sickness and rising above pain. As a rule they do, but if in exceptional cases one should fail, it is no reason for being disheartened. Let some other healer help you out, and rejoice that it occurs seldom.

Besides, this experience may be just what you need. Perhaps you are becoming egotistical, or are uncharitable toward the suffering. You must be made to feel continually that in your own strength you are nothing. One great mistake some make, which is the surest sign of failure, is to think one can believe for others and not for one's self. This is accepting it as theory instead of a truth.

The oil of joy is but as an anointing for a
nobler work. We shall have plenty to do, and
perhaps to bear. It will all be set before us, in
good time.

We need not die to go to God :
See how the daily prayer is given!
'Tis not across a gulf we cry,
"Our Father, who dost dwell in heaven!"

Dear friend, if it is true for your patient, it is true for yourself.

Don't tell your patient there is no need of pain and discord; that it is only a wrong way of thinking, and then take a sly dose of some material remedy, if you are laboring under some slight discord, quieting your conscience that it is the quickest way out of it, and thus better for the cause, as no one will know the difference. You are only cheating yourself.

Unless you apply the Truth to yourself you cannot apply it to others. It is so much easier to believe for others than for one's self. Many can easily see how the treatment might be good for some of their friends, but when it comes to considering its worth for themselves, it is another question. Therefore, I repeat, be honest with yourself, and by so doing deal honestly with God who meets you in your own soul. You are then fitted to deal Truth to others. You are not responsible for the way in which it is accepted. You have only to shed it, and God's law of love will mould the effect. It may not be in the way you expect, but that is nothing to you. Free your mind of all anxiety regarding the patient. Anxiety is doubt, and weakens the treatment.

Do not talk too much. Don't try to tell all you know at the first treatment.

It is often tiresome. As a rule, little talking is better. What you do say, make right to the point. Of course there are exceptional cases where more talking is necessary, but they are few.

Don't air your knowledge of big words. Be simple and modest. Don't say "I know I can cure you." Talk common sense in the plainest language possible, or, to put it all in a few words-don't be a crank.

It is only in the spiritual world that we truly live now; or are truly anything to each other.

Thought, The Motor

We do not wonder that St. Paul laid such stress upon charity; the charity that "thinketh no evil," for we are told by the wisest of all men that "as a man thinketh in his heart so is he." Not only so is he, himself, but so also are others. We earnestly wish every one could be made to understand the terrible power in thought. That they do not, is a prolific cause of misery. And yet hundreds of years before Christ, one of the principal tenets taught to a great portion of mankind, was the importance of "right thinking." For centuries since we have had the admonition, "watch and pray," but have not comprehended its full meaning.

It seems as if we are now eliminating the purest part of the teaching of all the world's great teachers, to assist us in realizing the importance of our thoughts, and give us a practical knowledge of how to use and control them. That the race does not understand this, brings them no exemption from suffering. On the contrary, through such experience only, will they learn. We are now speaking of the realm of thought called 'mortal mind" where all is error.

In reply to the remark that " we do not give expression to our best thoughts," one says: 'Not one tithe of the evil thoughts and desires in the world finds expression, in words and deeds." Perhaps not an immediate expression, but each one does find expression through its influence, which is two-fold, affecting those thought of, as well as the thinker. Each makes way for and encourages others like unto it, therefore each lowers the tone of the mind, and being all mind, this included the body.

The harmful effect is incalculable, for the Universe is like an electric wire, carrying and transmitting all the thoughts and desires poured into it, to other localities and persons; so these unbridled thoughts are like wild beasts let loose, and work much harm, for this is a deep and wide-spread influence, something more than a tearing of the flesh.

There are comparatively few who cannot be contaminated in some measure, by association, just as decaying fruit will affect all in close proximity to it.

When realize all this, it is almost a wonder that any resist it, until we have the new understanding. But like all epidemics, it is attracted to those in the condition to attract. Is it not as important to care for the mind, to avoid taking and spreading contagion, as for the body?

A thought of unkindness goes forth to give someone a feeling of depression he is not able to account for, and it as surely comes back as pain of head or body, weariness or weakness. When we feel ill, the first thing to do is to analyze our thoughts of the near past, and see if there were none we would like to recall.

Does it not then, behoove us to "keep watch and ward" over our thoughts; to allow none but kind, pure, and good ones to enter in, that none other may go out? In short to 'pray without ceasing," for in no other way can we "stand porter at the gate of thought."

If there was no way to escape the adverse influence the world would indeed be labyrinth of woe, and blasted by a thousand

Watch well your thoughts;
There all the danger lies.

Nero's. But there is a way. We learn that all this is a region of undeveloped, unenlightened "mortal mind" and has no power over us if we insist that it cannot have.

When we learn that there is a higher realm, more real, and just as near, just as accessible; that we are surrounded by Good, that it envelopes and will protect us like an armor; that 'there is no evil" unless our thoughts create it; when we learn that 'All is Good," that these so-called evil ways of thought are through ignorance, we can feel pity only, and a strong desire to enlighten all people. And it is easy after a little practice, and far more pleasant for ourselves, to so train our thoughts as to see only good in others, so there is no occasion for unkind thinking. It is wonderful

to find what can be done in this way. When any of the mortal tendencies arise, we can completely quell them in a few moments, for instance the sense of anger. We at once reason thus: "I am not angry; nothing can make me so, for I am one with Good and there is no anger. That was not the real Self of the person who said the words or did the deed. He is good and kind in reality, even though it does not so appear. I see it, for he too, is spirit, and one with the Infinite Spirit, Father of all, who created him pure and good; and my seeing this, will help to bring out the good that is within."

In a shorter time than it takes to tell, all trace of anger will be gone, and we shall feel light and happy. Is this not better than indulging hard bitter feelings?

The person too, will be more kind, less liable to annoy, just as surely as we try this plan in earnest. Such thoughts as these for our constant companions will build a better finer body for ourselves. We cannot prove it to you, but you can so easily prove it for yourself; just try. Is there a more blessed work than being messenger of peace and good? Truth "makes us free," but with a knowledge of Truth comes a great responsibility. We are "our brother's keeper."

Not only that, but if we allow thoughts of error, we are truly "forging a chain to bind ourselves with." When we have heard truth, we must take the consequences if we keep to the error. If we study our own thoughts for a few days, marking our feelings as they come and go, we need no teachings as to their importance.

Have you ever studied with Unity, Religious Science, or any other metaphysical tradition? Which? Ernest Holmes, Science of Mind

If so, what challenges does this lesson present to your previous understanding? None.

Are human beings co-creators with God? Explain your answer in detail.
God and I are one, therefore human being (spiritual beings) cannot co-create, but work as God. God works, through us and as us. All ideas come from God.

Can a practitioner reasonably feel righteous indignation toward someone or some action that appears to be evil? No, they cannot. A practitioner should be a loving, harmonious, spiritual being, because what is going on within the practitioner, will go towards the One receiving the treatment.

Does a practitioner ever think—or agree with a client or family member –
That death in a particular case is or would be a blessing? Discuss. I don't think that a practitioner would see death as blessing. They would, rather, say that the client might be a willing participant in their own transitioning.

Do human beings age degeneratively—grow bald, deaf, gray, arthritic,
Etc.? Discuss. I believe they age in the subconscious mind. It is how we feel about ourselves that allows us to age.

Write out the affirmative prayer that you could give for each of the
Following clients:

A man who has received a positive result on a test for the HIV virus.
I proclaim that there is One Power, and that Power is God. My life is God's life. My blood is God's blood, it circulates throughout my body, naturally flowing, as only Good. Every cell is an expression of God. Nothing has the power to come between me and my God, because we are One. The Kingdom is mine by divine right. I do not inherit sickness, for God is All. Good is what I seek and good is what I receive. I am vibrant, I am whole, perfect , and complete. And so it is.

A woman whose unmarried teen-age daughter has discovered she is pregnant.
I am Spirit, and am not governed by human conditions. My child is blessed with a precious gift from God, and this is a big blessing. As I look into my daughters eyes, I see God. I see God in my unborn grandchild. Spirit is my support, power, and strength. God is guiding me through this wonderful blessing, and I am thankful. All is well. And so it is.

An elderly woman who says she is blind in one eye and has been told by doctors that the sight in the other eye is going.
There is nothing with my vision. I can see clearly. I see with the vision of God. Human conditions have no place in my world. I do not inherit any sickness, because my eyes are God's eyes. I am youthful, whole, perfect, and complete. All is well. And so it is.

A couple about to be married.
Only the Love of God surrounds us. Our marriage is a sacred relationship blessed by God. Everywhere I walk I choose to see Love. As we make this commitment, we make a commitment to God, to love one another, and see the God within us. We are made whole by God, by joining together we become as one.

A man who—despite daily meditation and affirmative prayer on his own part as well as vigorous job hunting—has been unemployed for eighteen months and seems to be running out of resources.
My Perfect Job is right here now. There is nothing that can block me, no doubt, fear, anxiety, nothing. God is the only Power acting in my life. Every morning I awake and say thank you for my right and perfect job. God is the greatest provider, and I let go and let God knowing that my right job is right here, right now. I have a Divine Right, to the right and perfect job. There is no lack or limitation acting in my life. Supply flows naturally in my life because God is my substance.

Choose a current concern of your own and write an argumentative prayer on the subject every day until the matter is resolved (or at least for one month). All is possible with you Father, and I want some extra supply to do what needs to be done with Emma Curtis Hopkins. You are my Father, and all I have to do is ask, and know that you will help me out.

I want to help you, to cheer, strengthen and uplift- to send you on your daily pathway with perhaps a little more light and joy and courage. Let us consider more light and joy and courage. Let us consider for a moment the power of words.

We know that all through the Bible great importance is attached to the spoken word. Solomon said, "Who can measure the force of a right word?" "The words of the pure are pleasant words."

He recognized their power and continually spoke of the results of right and evil speaking. "A wholesome tongue is a tree of life, but perverseness of speech therein is a breach in the spirit." "Life and death are in the power of the tongue." If this be true we must look more to our language, consequently our thoughts, which give birth to our words.

Think of it friends! A true word spoken either by yourselves or others, is an elixir of strength and health; and influx of life itself. "He sent forth His word and healed them." He is sending it forth today. By who does He send it? By any who will speak it. You may be the happy messenger, or I, or some one in unknown silence. Rejoice that you may "minister and be ministered unto"--that you are privileged to say things that will bring life to yourself and all humanity, for the subtle chain of thought connects every one in the universe.

Live no longer in the foggy valleys of despair and doubt and weak complaints, but climb the sunny slopes of health and peace by the saying and thinking of words like the Master's which are "spirit and life." Up and onward! Leave the headaches and backaches, and chills and nervousness, in

NELLIE V. ANDERSO

VALIDS

the deep well of forgetfulness. No longer speak of them or acknowledge their being, but speak of the good, the beautiful, the true and desirable. Continually say the right words which shall be "like apples of gold in pictures of silver." Speak of health and happiness, of truth and goodness, of brightness and beauty. -as Paul so beautifully expresses it: "Whatsoever things are true, whatsoever things are honest, whatsoever things are just, whatsoever things are of good report...think on these things."

This is a sure rule. Try it. "You shall renew your strength; you shall mount up with wings as eagles." Why? Because you wait on the Lord. and you wait on the words of the Lord, no matter who says them." Wait patiently on the Lord and He shall give thee the desires of thine heart."

Blessed promises! How they comfort and help us; how they revive and cheer. Most precious thought of all, we may believe them, depend on them and find their echo in our own hearts. Because of the eager longing of hungry souls, there is a Divine answer. It is always ready for your reading, and when you have read yours, you help me to read mine. Its lines and pages are many and various, and like little children, we must learn the alphabet of this wonderful Book of Life; but we have a great and patient Teacher, and by passing the glad words along the line we shall soon be one in the magic bond of harmony and love, that wil yet redee, the world. "If ye abide in me, and my words abide in you, ye shall ask what ye will and it shall be done unto you."

Dear friends, be strong, fear not, and go on your way rejoicing.

LED TO

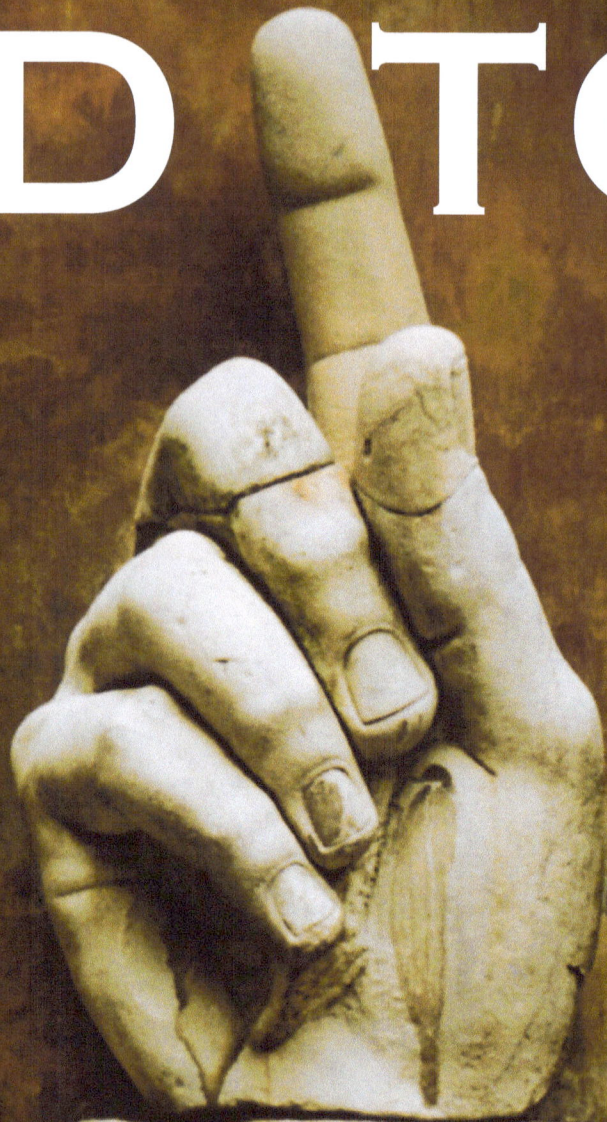

DO THIS WORK

"Go ye into all the world and preach the gospel, heal the sick." These were the words, several times repeated, that fell upon my ear, and sank deep into my heart while in the classroom two years ago. That was all I seemed to carry away with me of the beautiful lesson given us that day. Just before the lesson began, a clergyman had told the assembled class of wonderful healing done in his home by my teachers. He had taken a very thorough and practical course of instruction in medicine, (in England,) before studying for the ministry. He was amazed at the healing power that had been manifested in his family, when his experience told him his children were beyond aid.

He did not and could not understand, and was not able to accept the teachings of Christian Science, and concluded his speech by saying in an impressive manner, "I can preach the Gospel, but I cannot heal the sick." Can you wonder that a little later when the command came to me, I drew back and thought, "Who and what am I, that I should presume to do this work. if that man with his thorough training in two professions, his experience in both, cannot see the way to heal the sick as well as preach the Gospel, how can I, with my limited education, dulled by years of misuse and sickness, aspire to do both?" Four days this thought filled my mind, I was not able to put it aside even while in the classroom. Then when it seemed as if I could bear the conflict no longer, between the desire to drop the new way, from inability to do and be, and the impossibility not go on, I took my Bible, with the thought, this will show me the way, and the verse which came to me was, "Blessed are they which do hunger and thirst after righteousness, for they shall be filled."

Peace filled my heart. No more disquiet over that question has come to me. I was hungry and thirsty for righteousness and as the need arose I should be filled. No necessity to strive for knowledge in the way of the world, foolish to waste time in regret that I had it not in greater measure; be up and doing, and bread and water of life would be given me for self and those I must minister to.

Since that day I have not looked back. I grew slowly into the consciousness of Truth, for I had much to overcome, but I soon began to try to do for others. Gently have I been led on until a leading has come to me that I cannot set aside any more than I could that first command, "Go ye into all the world and preach the gospel, heal the sick." Little did I then think that I should be an instrument for so widely spreading the Truth that sets free, even "To all the world I must carry it."

Dear brother and sister scientists, I ask for your help and co-operation, not for myself, but for yourselves and all the world. I want you to feel that this magazine is yours, not mine. In its pages you shall find inspiration for yourselves, and the word that shall heal your patients. Here you can come with questions on any point that is not clear, and be answered. Here you shall be represented. Write out your thoughts; if they are true to science, the best shall be given to the world to heal and help others.

This little book put into the hands of your patients and students, shall help you in your work of healing and teaching. Every page shall be filled with healing potency. This magazine is dedicated to pure science and the interest of the scientists. I am not egotistical when I speak so highly of my little book, for I do not expect to write much for it myself, but to give you the thought of teachers and workers well known to you, and also a place for your own words. I have given up my sweet home life, a life of ease and comfort sacrificed desire for travel and pleasure, to do this work, and I confidently expect the cooperation of every scientist in the land.

Is it Jesus Or is it the Christ?

By Michael Terranova

I was licensed as a minister of the Teaching of the Inner Christ in 1979 and have taught prayer and meditation for many years. I have a conscious contact with that presence called Christ. The Christ is the same being we call our higher self. In the Hindu teaching it is called the Atman.

Jesus came into the world to make us aware of this Universal Presence, we call Christ. The founders of New Thought were very Christ based in their teachings. They applied the teachings of Jesus to make a practical and real system so the followers of their teachings could live a full and prosperous life.

Charles Fillmore named his organization Unity School of Christianity and taught the same Truth Jesus did.

Ernest Holmes was once asked by a traditional Christian minister, "how come so many of our members come to your church" and he said, "Maybe it is because we **live** Jesus' teachings."

It is not Jesus that is the Truth of our beings but the Christ. Many people are plugged in by the name of Jesus because of past experiences with Christianity. In my opinion it would be good to heal anything about a name or word taking us into a denial mentatility. My mother-in–law is Italian as am I. She gets upset when someone says Dago; well I have made a point to say it jokingly with her. She has now let go of the charge she had on it. May anyone that has a charge on the name Jesus let go, too.

Following are some quotes from Ernest Holmes.

"To think of Jesus as being different from other men is to misunderstand his mission and purpose in life. He was a way-shower and proved his way a correct one. His method was direct, dynamic and powerful, yet extremely simple and easy to comprehend. He believed in God, in himself, as Power and Reality. Believing in God within, he was compelled to believe in himself.

Jesus was a man, a human being, who understood his own nature. He knew that as the human embodies the divine it manifests the Christ Nature. Jesus never thought of himself as different from others: his whole teaching was that what he did others could do.

We must not look afar to see the Christ, for he is ever near at hand. He is always within us. To the individual there can never be any power, truth or life, unless he is able to realize and recognize it.

I have been studying with Rev. Marcia Sutton for about 10 years and I asked her to comment on this idea. Here is what she had to say, "Previously I have spoken about the importance of realizing that what was flowing through the man Jesus was more significant than the doctrines that evolved out of his historical life. And what moved through him was the Living Presence of God that is the Light of Christ. Remember, Jesus said that the Light of Divine Radiance that was in him is in us. That is to say, it moves through us to the degree that we identify with It and become It through real spiritual practice. The promise is that each of us shall become a Light unto the World. I think this promise is real for us right now and it is already happening. It happens each time we gather together in worship and group spiritual practice. It takes place every time we lay down judgments and accusations about others, the world and ourselves. It takes place every time we see through the power of appearances and seek to understand the spiritual message behind every experience. It takes place every time we turn away from the pull of the world and listen for the sweet call of Spirit."

Mary Manin Morrissy of the Living Enrichment Center said, "We are New Thought Christians", meaning we are called as New Thoughters to live the teachings that Jesus brought to the world.

"Knock and the door will be opened, seek and ye shall find, and the Truth will set you free." Mt 7:7

Christ is waiting for us to make the move.

Problems are ANGELS

By Rev. Patrice Julien

In my work as a Minister I get a lot of mails or calls from people who face « problems » and want to get rid of them. They expect a fast « fix », a prayer that will solve everything on their behalf... Sometimes, they get a result about that specific problem but, after a while, I hear again from them about a new problem... We could go endlessly from one problem to the next if we do not ask ourselves the question: « What is a problem? » and « To what does the problem point? ».

Nobody really likes problems... That is the good point about it. It is like a little piece of rock in our shoes. It is disturbing. See, we were walking without even noticing it and suddenly, something attracts our attention...That is the « friendly » function of problems...They CALL our attention on something... We may have had other calls, lighter ones, but we may have let them go unanswered, like the sound of an alarm clock when we feel we don't want to wake up...Problems work like alarm clocks. The level of the sound is programmed to get louder and louder...That is the reason why certain people show up in my office after a « light call » when others wait until things get really bad.

Once awakened by the problem, the next point is to answer the question : "To what does the problem point?". The answer is always the same, it is always about our IDENTITY. It always point to the eternal question "Who do I believe I Am?" It is where meeting the teachings of Emma Curtis Hopkins can lead us to a very practical process of

"restoration" of our True Self.

The first Step of the process she sets up is called the "Statement of Being". It is based on the observation that everywhere in nature there is an "inbuilt" orientation towards what we may call "our Good". She writes: "At the word that there is Good for everyone and everyone ought to have Good, each mind agrees" Scientific p. 21. Praying then is not about trying to bend the will of God to satisfy our selfish desires, it is about stating a Truth: "There is Good for everyone..." Not there "should be": "There IS".

So then, why do problems appear? How can we get separated from our Good when the promise is that "we ought to have it"...? This apparent contradiction gives us the Good start. The answer to the "Why" is that we have inherited two identities, one from Life itself, naturally programmed to bring us our Good and another inherited from our "cultures" built on a strong belief in a separation from the unconditional Source of all supply. Our traditions, our educations and our religions have taught us a false distinction between human and divine, good and bad, spiritual and material, creating a war within our consciousness...That is the cause of all problems...

Emma writes in the first chapter of Scientific Christian Mental Practice : "If you have a clear idea of how sweet life, free and unburdened, must be, look to this science to bring you this life. And declare plainly that sweet, free life is our Good." Sounds too simple isn't it ? Hard to believe that this can be enough to clear out all our problems...

This "hard to believe" is the true problem...We have unconsciously built such a strong belief in a false identity that we feel some resistance to let it go... People tend to stick to their problem whatever they are. A sickness, a financial issue, a conflict ,..., they consider it as "reality". By doing so they lock themselves behind an illusory door when they could realize instantly that they are free, right now . It would take only an unbreakable faith in the statement that if there is Good for us Now, the apparent contradiction creating the pain have no reality...

By nature, the solution is NOW

because the problem itself is an illusion, a filter masking the light. The light is not affected, the only thing affected is our perception...So if the problem can vanish instantaneously, why do we sometimes need so much time to get things on the right track? Just because of our conscious or unconscious resistance to the Truth of our Identity. How many persons on this planet are ready to believe that all what we call "information" from newspapers to TV news and Internet is the reflection of an hypnotic belief in our false identity? Very few. Quantum Physics have already given us all the proofs that Reality is generated by states of consciousness but we still continue to hold on an outdated conception of a "solid reality" independent of the nature our thoughts... That is the reason why problems seem to generate more and more problems. We try to solve them on the level of our "false identity" when their presence itself is the Call back to our true Identity.

But don't worry, in fact the Good works well. The good news is that we finally have no choice.

Sooner or later the pain generated by the problems will bring us out of our illusory belief system. We will have to become our own Moses, and go in quest of our true Self. If pain become too unbearable we will take the rod of the Statement of Being and open the seas of illusions created by our beliefs. To make the job easier we have to remember that every problem is at the shadow of a lie we have believed in. Finding the pain reveals the lie. And, exciting promise, behind the lie we will always find a long awaited Good belonging to us...Behind every pain, every frustration, every problem lies a precious gem belonging to us by Divine Sonship. Finding our treasure may be instantaneous (if we are still able to be like children looking after Easter eggs in a garden) or it may take a more or less long period of cleansing depending on our resistance to Truth. Anyway, I suggest to take the "Scientific Christian Mental Practice" of ECH as a travel guide for the journey...And during your journey remember, apart of your Good all deceptive appearances are just illusions...

I AM ME

I AM ME

EVERYTHING THAT I AM SUPPOSED TO BE

I AM THE LIGHT OF THE WORLD

I AM THE POWER THAT NEVER FAILS

I AM NEVER DEFEATED

I MOVE MOUNTAINS

I GROW AND GROW

I AM BEAUTIFUL IN EVERY WAY

I AM SPIRIT

I CAN ONLY BE MOVED BY THE HAND OF GOD

I AM ME

-Natalie Jean

Dream, spirituality & Medicine... The Mugwort Power.

-Julien Andrieu-Franceschetti

Compositae
(Anthemideae)

Artemisia vulgaris L.

As an energy and spiritual healer, a gift from my family for more than 6 generations, I use different tools, elements, object, stones and herbs. One of my favorite is the Mugwort, Artmesia Vulgaris L. , known also under the name of Moxa, Artemis Herb, Felon Herb, Muggons, Old Man, Sailor's Tobacco.
 I use it as a medicinal plant, for spiritual practice, as incense and also you can use it to cook… Artemisia vulgaris L. (latin name) is native to temperate Europe, Asia, northern Africa, Alaska and is naturalized in North America, grows almost everywhere around the world. Mugwort grows in high-elevation pastures, forest edges, valleys, hillside wasteland, ditches, and roadsides.
 She is from Asteraceae or compositae family like Marigold, Echinacea, Yarrow, Dandelion and many more… Plants in Asteraceae are medically important in areas that don't have access to Western medicine. Tea, tincture, compress can be made to use for different healing process.
Used for centuries as an alternative medicine,
it is antibacterial, anthelmintic, anti-inflammatory, antiseptic, antispasmodic, carminative, cholagogue, diaphoretic, digestive, diuretic, emmenagogue, expectorant, hemostatic, nervine, purgative, stimulant, stomachic, and tonic, cleansing toxins from the blood. An infusion of the leaves and flowering tops is used in the treatment of all matters connected to the digestive system, it increases stomach acid and bile production, eases gas and bloating, improving digestion, the absorption of nutrients and strengthening the entire digestive system. It is used in alternative medicine to expel intestinal worms, nervous and spasmodic affections, asthma, sterility, functional bleeding of the uterus and menstrual complaints, and diseases of the brain. As a gargle for sore throat, a wash for sores and a poultice for infections, tumors and to stop bleeding.
Caution: Should not be used by pregnant women since it can cause a miscarriage.

Mugwort can grow to 4 ft tall, but usually remains around 1 or 2 ft high. It branches towards the top into many spikes of small greenish flowers. The leaves are alternate, green on the top and white and fuzzy on the bottom. The lower leaves are finely dissected with pointed lobes, while the upper leaves usually have three or so lobes, some of the smallest near to the top being linear. The leaves and flowering stalks should be gathered just at blossoming time, usually between July and early September. The root is gathered after the flowering time in late autumn. The root is washed and dried and the leaves and flowering stalks dried in a dry and dark and warm place.

Through the part below I tried to give you a general explanation about the medicinal use and effect of the plant. In the second part, I will tell you more about the spiritual aspect and use of it, witchcraft and hoodoo be ready !

Mugwort is considered a sacred herb of Artemis, the Greek goddess of the moon, the hunt, and chastity, which gives it its scientific name. Sacred to the Druids, It is one of the nine magical herbs of the Druidic and Anglo-Saxon tribes and was associated with protection of travelers and with fertility rites. This plant is connected to the Moon, planetary Venus and the Copper metal. It enhances dreams, especially of the prophetic sort, helps with lucid dreaming, and aid in astral travel and generally with out-of-body experiences. This magic herb can be stuffed into dream pillows or drunk as a tea for dream enhancement. Along similar lines, it is often utilized to consecrate and dress instruments for divination, like crystal balls.

The Native American tribes used it as a smudging herb to clear and cleanse sacred space. Also they equate mugwort with witchcraft. They believed that the rubbing of the leaves on the body are said to keep ghosts away, and a necklace of mugwort leaves is said to help protect against dreaming about the dead.

Roman soldiers were known to put mugwort in their sandals to keep their feet from getting tired. It has been believed that John the Baptist wore a girdle of mugwort in the wilderness for protection. Other magical attributes include the protection for road weary travelers, and general protection against the evils of the spirit realms.

What can you do with mugwort:

It can be taken as a tea or smoked before bedtime, branches can be hung near the bed, or the crushed leaves and flowers can be put in a sachet or pillow to place on or near the bed As a tea, daily one or two cups, by fever each four hour half a cup.

To make a tincture, use a masson jar, put ¼ of dry herbs and fill up the jar with brandy or vodka. Leave it for 40 days minimum and strain it and put the liquid in a small bottle with dropper. Use the tincture, three times daily 2 to 5 ml , 1 full dropper 3 time the day. For fatigue or tiredness chew slowly on three or four leaves. Combine mugwort 1:2 with white sandalwood to make a mugwort incense.

The leaves of Mugwort are used for stuffing's. It can also be used in stew- and meat dish. To make incense yourself (all Artemisia kinds are suitable) you pick the buds, just before they get into bloom. Make pieces of equal length (approximately 15 cm) and let them dry for approximately two days. Make a bundle of 2.5 cm diameter and bind them together with a cotton rope (do not use artificial fiber). Light from one side, close the flame and let the bars smoulder.

I hope that will give you a good idea of what mugwort is, how to use it and her spiritual properties. Don't be afraid if you have a weird dream, its normal! It s also good idea to skip a few days, don't drink mugwort tea every night, taking a break for 3 or 4 days might help you to have more good dream when you start drinking the tea again, this is my personal experience.

Please respect nature, when you harvest mugwort cut the plant properly and leave the roots in the soil. That way you give the plant the chance to grow again and again. Feel free to talk to her and tell her why and what you will do with her later, she will appreciate it and give it back to you as a good energy when you use it for spiritual or medicinal use.

Don't forget, every plant, herbs are alive like us, they sleep, they wake up, they have their own day and go back to sleep. Treat them like a part of you, like something precious and learn what they have to teach you. Plants are powerful in different ways, that it can take a life work to learn about them, so let the journey begin...

http://www.facebook.com/ julian.franceschetti
energyhealingandshamanism

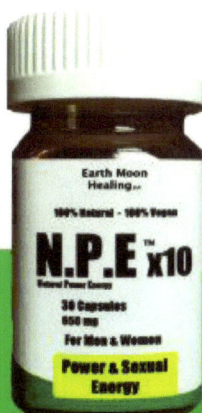

SEEDS

Under the Haitian Sun are many children in Need of your support. A great deal can be done with your contribution. A gift goes a long way and opens many doors that were once closed.

Enrich a child's life.

Be the key.

Plant your Seeds.

SEEDS-HAITI, Inc. is a non-profit charitable organization that was created in 1987 to provide assistance the Haitian people in their rebuilding efforts. However, our main focus resides in educating the youth. In the aftermath of the January 12, 2010, SEEDS-Haiti, Inc. adopted and rebuilt the Institution Mixed Emanuel Bon Samaritain de Digue Probably primary school that was damaged by the quake. The school is located in Arcahaie, Haiti. SEEDS helps the school by providing teacher salaries and other immediate necessities. The organization also needs to provide at least one meal a day, school uniforms and supplies, add enhancing courses to the curriculum by building new classrooms and hire more teachers. Help us fulfill our mission by supporting our programs. Please visit **seedshaitiinc.com** to make your tax deductible contribution or mail your check to **SEEDS-HAITI, Inc., P.O. Box 66524, Washington, D.C. 20035.**

Infinite Me

Awakes

Get thi
Reveal

Custom D

888.761.0388
infinite-elevation.com

s done.

ur truth.

gn Services

Publishing

Branding

Promotional Events

Advertising/ Marketing

Stationery

Cr8ive Design

infinit∞levation™

SIGNIFICANT
SATURN

BY PERVENIA P BROW

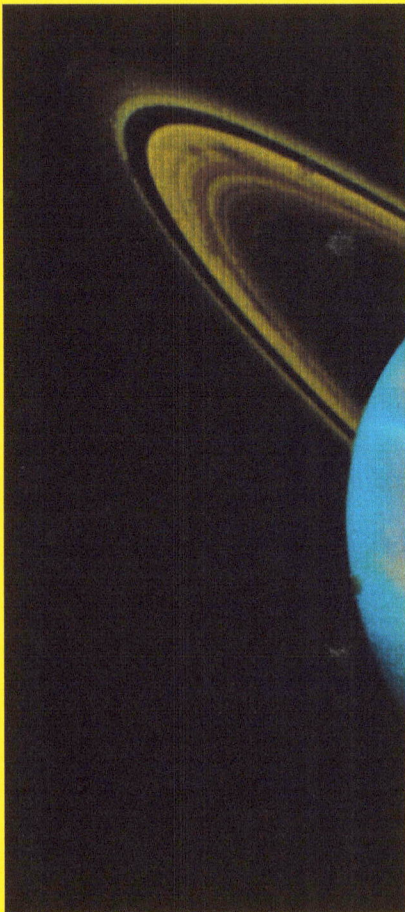

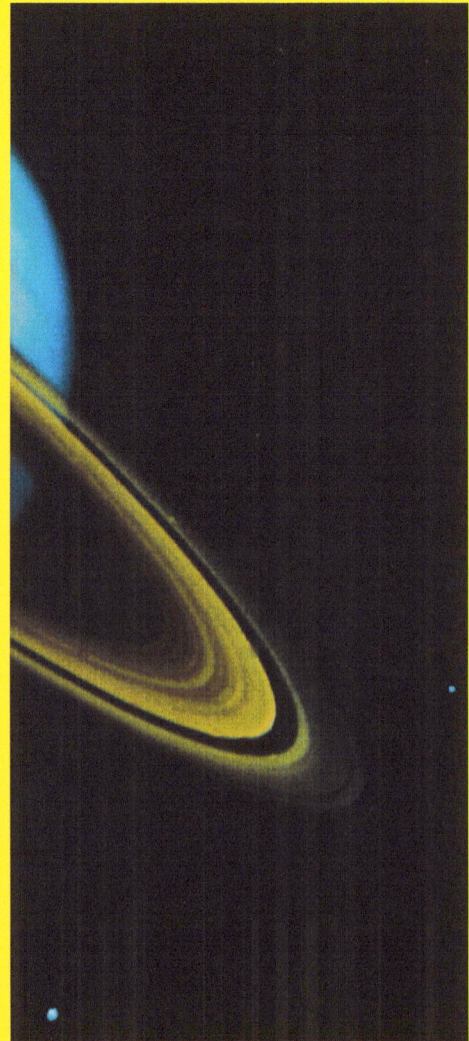

Where is Saturn? Subtle signs prompting lifestyle changes could be obvious indicators.

Saturn, the Taskmaster, notoriously nestles in multiple sun signs simultaneously. And that's fine, so long as awareness of its presence and reasons for its visits are clear. Otherwise, confusion may complicate plans and create a turbulent cosmic forecast.

Not to be undermined, Saturn's significance is key to understanding "our astrological sign [as] the vehicle through which our consciousness travels to realize our highest potential." This pertinent planet is so much more than a Teacher and a Tester. It is a rewarder of patience and effort. Sensing its stimulus (as we all do) could mean Saturn's about to pay you a visit. This might be a good time to review your cosmic itinerary and prepare your astrological houses for a dignitary visit.

AQUARIUS

1.20-2.18

For much of 2012, Saturn will dwell in your 9th House of Big Ideas enhancing your symbolic insight and stimulating intellectual growth. You thrive intellectually in faraway places, where you are free to live life as you choose—on your own terms. In your 9th House, this Saturn brings clarity and understanding to many of your past experiences, while challenging you to discipline impatience and channel it optimistically.

PISCES

2.19-3.20

Saturn has occupied your 8th House of Shared Resources since October 29, 2009. Abiding in your 8th House, the Taskmaster's lesson is expression of feelings to develop inner empowerment. Honest communication strengthens and deepens your relationships creating the intimacy you desire. However, until you're done playing the despondent damsel, Saturn won't reward you with the confidence and power that honest communication brings.

ARIES

3.21-4.19

On October 5, Saturn will check-out of Cancer and Virgo and check-in to Aries' 8th House of Intimacy, where Saturn aims to teach you to overcome dependency on others and to trust your own inner guidance. Until Saturn is convinced you've made sincere efforts in this regard, desire for power will remain unattainable.

TAURUS

4.20-5.20

Novice no more. Saturn moves to your 7th House of Partnerships on October 5, encouraging you to assume authority and act with decisiveness in your relationships. How you relate to others is crucial to getting the respect you deserve. Avoid shifting responsibility for yourself onto others. Saturn's 7th House lesson is all about reciprocity in your relationships

GEMINI

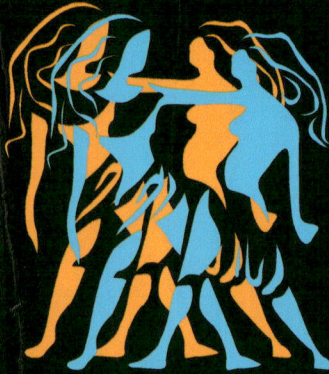

5.21-6.21

Saturn journeys to your 11th House of Dreams on October 10, directing your focus in contributions to society. Saturn is aware of your durability, maturity, and creativity. The Ruler of Responsibility expects you to step up to the plate, accept your assignment, and use your interpersonal skills to make positive impacts in your community and social groups. Unless you fulfill Saturn's 11th House curriculum, this lesson will recur as karmic carryover.

CANCER

6.22-7.22

Restoring harmony is the reason for Saturn's visit to your 4th House of Security. Achieving domestic tranquility promotes emotional security. And, when you experience the balance of these calming qualities, you're completely fulfilled! Saturn's 4th House lesson teaches you—if you're open to learning it—that harmony lies within self-acceptance, not a set of outmoded rigid rules

LEO

7.23–8.22

Saturn has resided in your 3rd House of Communication since October 29, 2009. What does this mean for Leo? Intellectual development! Expect encounters or experiences that challenge you in the areas of learning and/or education. Saturn's visit to your 3rd House is prompts you to "earn intellectual authority" by increasing mental adeptness and responsibility. High demands! No worries. There will be plenty of opportunities to learn this lesson, as Saturn extends it tenancy through October 5.

VIRGO

8.23–9.22

Saturn's prolonged residency in your 2nd House of Self-Worth began July 21, 2010. Saturn continues its observant occupancy until October 5. While residing in your 2nd House, the watchful Taskmaster assesses how you acquire material wealth, which is inextricably linked to self-worth and helps you develop an uncompromising.

LIBRA

9.23–10.22

Give yourself permission to be who you are. *Tune out external criticism!* That's the purpose of Saturn's visit to your 5th House of Personality. Don't wait for others to give you a well-deserved applause. Bask in your accomplishments and shower yourself with feelings of appreciation. Convince the Taskmaster you are courageous and confident and Saturn will stamp your lesson—*LEARNED!*

SCORPIO   SAGITTARIUS   CAPRICORN

10.23-11.21   11.22-12.21   12.22-1.19

Concluding its journey in your 12th House of Endings on October 5, Saturn polishes up your relationships and paves the way for new beginnings. This fresh start creates opportunities to develop new encounters and experiences with others, if you can truly forgive previous offenses and disappointments. Until you do, the sense of inner accomplishment you crave may continually elude you.

On October 10, Saturn begins its two-year tenure in your 12th House of Endings. *Translation*: this is a time of spiritual cleansing and healing. Saturn is here to teach forgiveness, especially of those who could not or did not provide the safety and security sought during your childhood years. You must compassionately embrace those who abandoned you in order to heal your emotions.

Changing of the guard: Saturn transitions from your 10th House of Career to your 11th House of Groups on October 5. The primary purpose of your ruling planet, Saturn, in your 11th House is "collaboration and cooperation." Opportunities to adhere to Saturn's rules and requirements could mean the difference between career advancement or stagnation. It is imperative to work as part of a team to accomplish goals during Saturn's 11th House visit and find a way to integrate this quality into your character. Otherwise, the success you seek may become elusive, if not impossible.

THE GREAT PHILOSOPHER, SENECA, SAID, "IT TAKES A LIFETIME TO LEARN HOW TO LIVE." THANKFULLY, SATURN PROVIDES MULTIPLE OPPORTUNITIES.

"I AM NOT AFRAID THAT MY PEACE WILL BE DISTURBED."

EMMA CURTIS HOPKINS

The regular monthly meeting of the Hopkins Metaphysical Association was held July 31, 1888, at the C.S. Bureau Rooms, McVicker's Building. Meeting was called to order by the President, who prefaced the usual silent prayer byt the following words:

"If it were not for apprehension and fearfulness, we should never be weak or sickly or unhappy. The mortal quivers with terror lest health fail, misfortune overtake, or friends desert. We can hardly find however, a single mind steadfastly willing to take the scientific and true way to boldness and fearlessness."

What is the scientific way? even the scientists are asking. Why, "pray as if you had already" been set free from fear. How is that? Say vehemently, "I am not afraid." Did you ever hear how the ancients tried to teach the people to be fearless and strong and satisfied?

They did not seem to love the Origin or Principle upon which the practical working rested, but they taught that the very air is charged with an etheric substance which no sense can fix, describe or experience. It is like plastic wax to the strong vehement thought, and will come back to whoever speaks a strong thought.

"Put away your old fears and stand free to receive your inheritance of strength and power," they urged.

Now science explains that this putting away meant denial. The Western mind revolts at denial. But Oh! the sweet freedom that comes with earnest denial! Let us set asider our positive prejudice and be true to true science for a few minutes. Let us unite in silent prayer to set us forevermore free from wrong and evil. Say with me in the silence, these words:

I am not afraid that my health will fail me.

I am not afraid that my strength will leave me.

I am not afraid that my peace will be disturbed, from henceforth forevermore.

"I will fear no evil, for Thou art with me." Amen.

Mrs. Stacy, our usual leader in singing being absent, that part of our exercises was conducted by Mrs. Nina B. Hughes, who at the suggesting of the president led the members in the hymn, 'All hail the power of Jesus' name." It was sung with much feeling after the relation of an anecdote by Mrs. Hopkins about an army, that, after a long, hard march were tired and discouraged, when the band commenced to play this dear old hymn. In a minute they were changed and moved on to victory with renewed courage and strength, inspired by the familiar hymn.

The reading of minutes of June meeting followed; were approved and accepted. President introduced Rev. W.W. Clayton of Lansing, Mich., who favored the meeting with a pleasing little talk upon the two phases of science, the theoretical and practical.

Mrs. Hughes had been out in the field teaching and told some of her experiences. She found that people outside had very few right and true ideas concerning Christian Science. She thought we had as yet not the remotest idea of the power of mind. Mr. A.S. Field told of some of his experiences in healing in St. Joseph, Mich.

The regular monthly lecture by the President before the association, was as follows, as nearly as possible to report at this date:

It is very plain that not much talk on the part of Christian Scientists, is the wise plan of action now. Silence and silent work to prove the power of the science, and our sincere interest in it, we must maintain.

There are intense feelings stirring all classes of minds-intense feelings which spoken words would betray, and hurt others if uttered. The silence always them. The silence brings judgment to administer upon them. The silence moves wisdom to utter right and potent words, quite unlike the passions of grief, anger, disappointment, resentment, that choked us before.

So many people are grieved--so many are disappointed--so many are angered. These are faculties undirected. They are good signs. They are energies you ought to harness like servants to your bidding. Take anger that shakes you like a reed in the wind. In the heat of your anger, treat some sluggish paralytic. See! You are not angry at him; you are not angry at your companion or friend, or one who has wronged you, and so the excitement is stirring and quickening of functions to him, the innocent. You soon forget the anger you felt at the friend in your strength of silent treatment.

O the enfeebling prostration of disappointed hopes! How can you treat to help others you think, when you are in despair yourself? How out of paralysis of judgment raise wise words?

You are greater than the disappointment. Did not you know that? Rise in the silence, like a bold, young lion, and cry vehemently over the silent airs, that you are greater than your circumstances and greater than your disappointment. Say these words till you warm to new life, and new hope, and new judgment. There is another way. If you can sleep when you are disappointed, the disappointment will go past your door, and in the silence of sleep the Law will write the cheering word upon your heart.

We must prove ourselves greater than mortal mind and all its conditions and circumstances. What good is it to be really greater if we do not prove it? Do not let us talk the science for a while.

Let us be scientific.

You are puzzling over three questions just now:

1. What does it mean to take no thought of what we shall eat or drink, when Jesus himself fasted forty days, and the wise men of Scripture fasted oft and dieted to suit occasions?

2. How is the science consistent when in one breath it tells us we can have nothing to ourselves, and in the next breath tells us we can have the desire of our hearts?

3. When we do not know exactly what course to pursue, how can we be sure it is the true or false self that urges us into doing a certain way?

These are very good questions and cover a great deal of ground. First.-What does it mean to take no thought, etc.? The apparently contradictory nature of word and action here is the divinest harmony to the true scientist. You certainly must not take the least bit of care about what you eat, drink or wear, and yet you are to eat, drink and dress always properly.

Cast all your care-that is, let his Friend so close by you take the care on His own shoulders. Go you about healing in His name, teaching the truth as far as you know it; preaching silently or audibly, as judgment dictates, all about the glory and beauty and blessedness of Spiritual Reality.

"Seek ye first the kingdom of God and His righteousness, and all these things shall be added." That is, if you are dealing with spiritual doctrines, the material movements and things will set themselves right. You are not to set the material things and movements right in order to be spiritual, but you are to be spiritual in order to set material things right.

If you are spiritually minded you will often fast many days and not realize it. You do not fast in order to be spiritual, but fast because you are spiritual. Fasting in order to be spiriual, weakens you. It is a taking thought for the body that is forbidden. But fasting that you do when you are already spiritual, strengthens and invigorates you.

You have meat to eat during those hours that the world knows of. Jesus fasted because he became spiritual as a reward for preaching and teaching Truth. So did the wise men. Then ate again after the fast. He took no care about it. The Law worked its own way through him and with him.

We must be spiritual by thinking and telling spiritual Truth, Then we shall find food, raiment and shelter provided and suited for us.

Second.-- You ask how the science is consistent which tells us we can have nothing, and then says we can have all things? I find that I must scream, vehemently shout, or whisper mysteriously, or whatever way will impress upon you that nothing, nothing, worse than nothing, belongs to mortality. But all things belong to the spiritual, or truly minded.

Some are hounding me as if I originated the statement of Scripturem that the fulfillment of the desire of the heart belongs by right to everyone of us. But I only read out of the Law, I do not originate. I did not discover it, Here is the text again which is the key to the whole question: "Seek ye first the kingdom...and all these things shall be added." Renounce the world the flesh and the devil. That is, deny their reality. Then spiritual powers and spiritual faculties, and spiritual supplies make you a new creature. Think what is orderly, true, divine. Speak of these things, teach them; then you will say the mountains of sorrow, Be gone! and sorrows shall flee away. You shall say to desolation, "I am not desolate," and true companionship will come to you. You shall have more abundantly than you can ask or even think after you have become truly spiritual. Not till then. To the materially-minded nothing is promised. To the spiritually-minded all things are promised.

The desire you have this moment deep down in your heart

MA

EMMA

RTIS

CURTIS

OPKINS

HOPKINS

you ought to have fulfilled. Being your own it ought to come to you.

"Rise the hills, And swim the sea, And like thy shadow Fall on thee."

But it wont come till you are scientific-speak Truth.

It is very strange how our desires change when we become truthful. We set out denying all the obstacles that keep us from getting our wishes. Barrier after barrier is removed by our denials. Then suddenly we take a new outlook. We would not have the thing we first asked for now. Our wishes lie along quite another channel. We see things from a more sensible standpoint. We finally get just what we desire. Not what we first asked for, but just what we have come to want. The first desire was a good thing to start off with. The last one to end up with. "We shall be changed."

Third.-- You ask how to tell the true monition from the false one? Easy enough. Do that which seems just right, or what you seem driven to do and trust your choice. Trust that the Best, the Divine, guided you. Never mind how far away from the Right it seems. Trust that it is Right. Oh! how "you" do like to be trusted! That is, the "you" likes to be trusted by what seems to be you. Trust the Leading. It is the Divine of you. Fear not. Trust. Trust. Trust. Each hour of trusting "yourself" brings you out clearer and clearer as the off-spring of Wisdom. If I were as afraid as so many seem to be, I should be quite swamped, because so many condemn me for the bold moves I make. But I jump to a Leading, and let my best beloved cry out against it. Nobody is quite so wise concerning your own matters as yourself. Whatever you do while trying to do the best you can, you have a right to believe in doing. I know this by experience. I know it by Law. I know it by inspiration.

The business of the day followed. Miss Brady, of the membership committee, reported favorably upon the names presented for membership at June meeting. It was voted that they be made members and cordially welcomed.

Executive Committee reported that at the present juncture no outside work had better be attempted. Mrs. Talbot's resignation of the office of treasurer on account of prolonged absence, was reported by the secretary, and accepted with thanks for past services and regrets at withdrawal. Mrs. Sarah S. Kelting was elected to fill the vacancy.

Mrs. Hughes of the Student's Aid Committee, reported having given aid to man. President spoke of the need of all going to work somewhere, not sitting idly down. Chicago need Science workers as much as outside cities. No one knows how much, or well, he or she can do until they try. Several have gone out are doing well healing and teaching. One especially, an exceptionally quiet woman, is making a stir of interest in the Science. Remember, the race is not awalys to the swift, nor the battle of the strong. Small beginnings seem discouraging, but work for all you are worth and more will be given you.

Meeting adjourned to August 28th.

Ida A. Nichols, Secretary.

EMMA

CURTIS

HOPKINS

EMMA

CURTIS

HOPKI

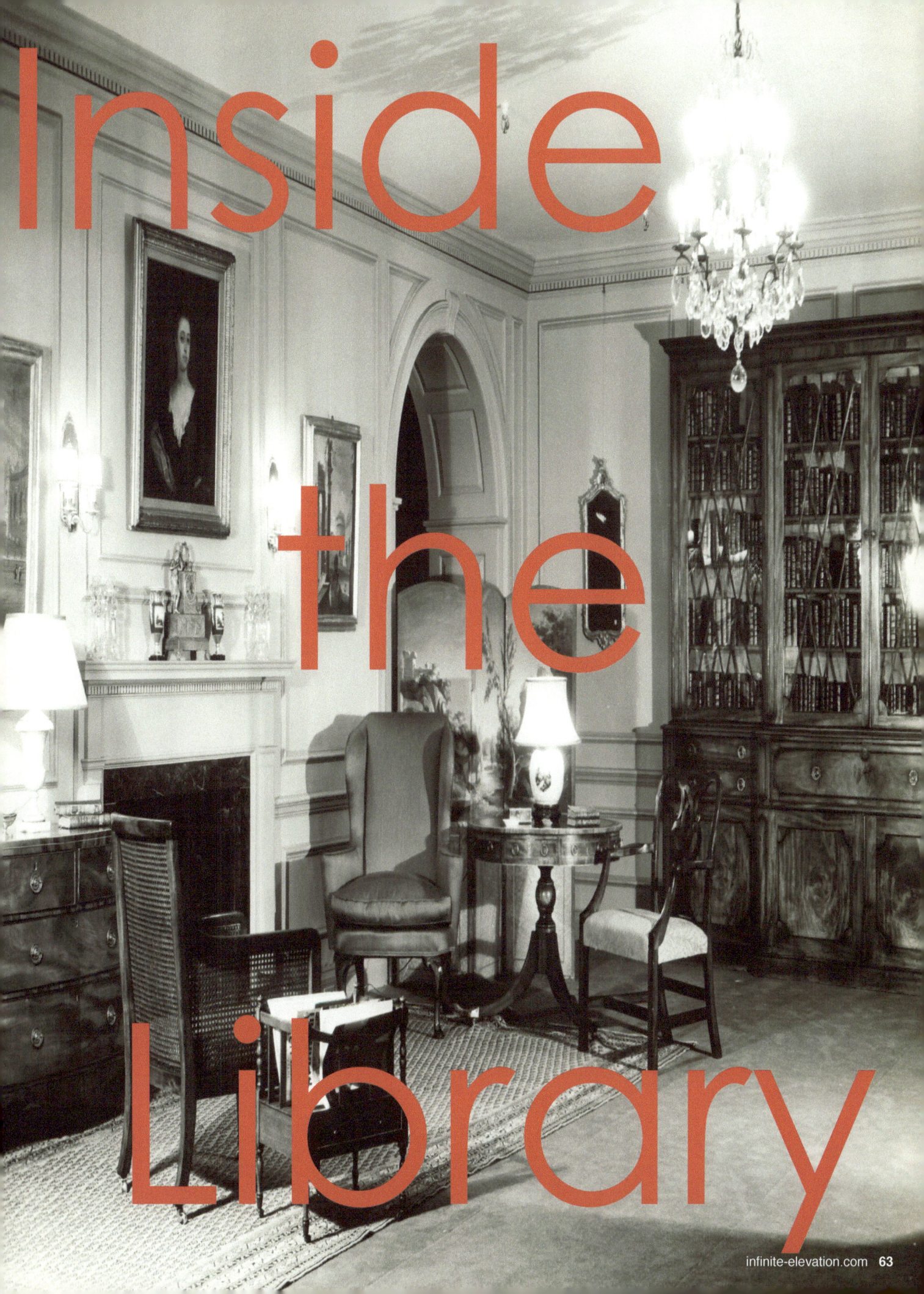

Inside

the

Library

BIBLE INTERPRETATIONS

FIRST SERIES

July 5 - September 27, 1891

EMMA CURTIS HOPKINS

BIBLE INTERPRETATIONS

SECOND SERIES

October 4 - December 27, 1891

EMMA CURTIS HOPKINS

BIBLE INTERPRETATIONS

THIRD SERIES

January 3 - March 27, 1891

EMMA CURTIS HOPKINS

BIBLE INTERPRETATIONS

FOURTH SERIES

April 3 - June 26, 1892

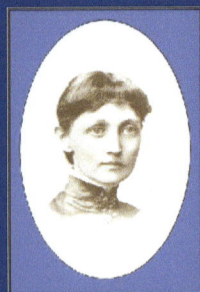

EMMA CURTIS HOPKINS

BIBLE INTERPRETATIONS

FIFTH SERIES

July 3 - September 18, 1892

EMMA CURTIS HOPKINS

BIBLE INTERPRETATIONS

SIXTH SERIES

September 25 - December 18, 1892

EMMA CURTIS HOPKINS

Bible Interpretation Series 1-12

Bible Interpretation Series by
Emma Curtis Hopkins

"There are many books written on the teachings of the Bible, but none can touch the surface of the true messages more than these Bible interpretations. With each word you can feel and see how Spirit spoke through Emma. The mystical interpretations take you on a wonderful journey to Self Realization."

EMMA CURTIS HOPKINS

DROPS
of
GOLD

EMMA CURTIS HOPKINS

ESOTERIC

PHILOSOPHY

Deeper Teachings
in
Spiritual Science

EMMA CURTIS HOPKINS

THE
GOSPEL
SERIES

EMMA CURTIS HOPKINS

HIGH WATCH

HIGH
MYSTICISM

STUDIES IN
THE WISDOM
OF THE SAGES
OF THE AGES

EMMA CURTIS HOPKINS

JUDGMENT
SERIES
IN
SPIRITUAL
SCIENCE

EMMA CURTIS HOPKINS

SELF TREATMENTS
involving
THE RADIANT I AM

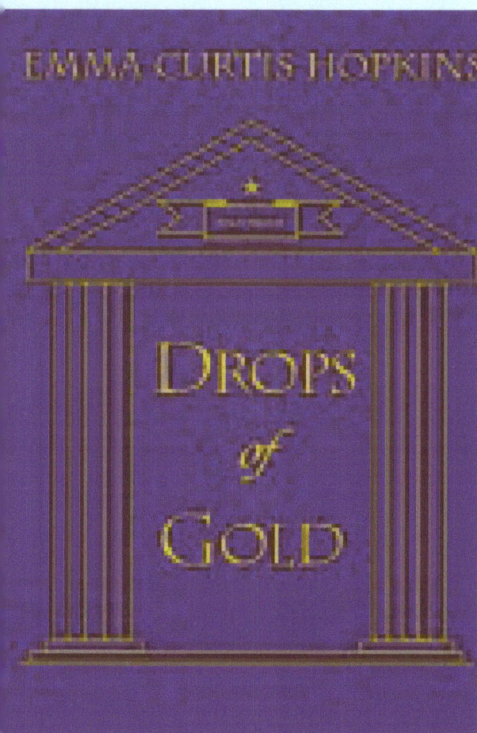

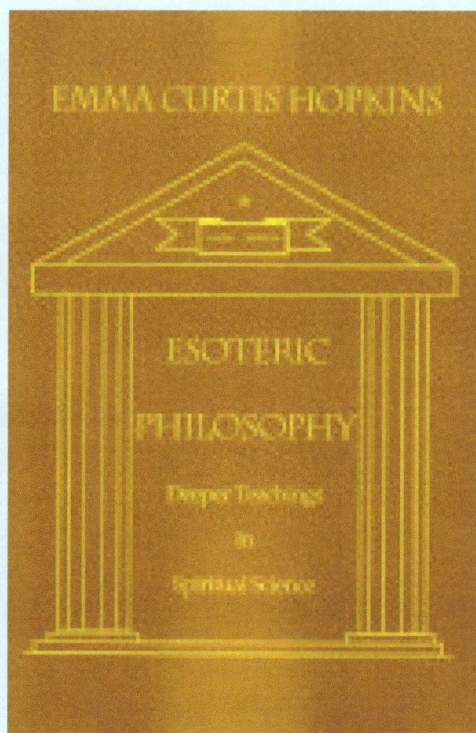

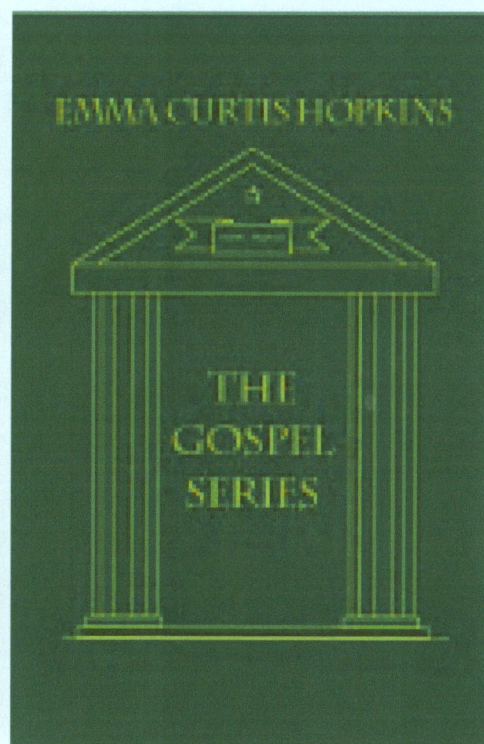

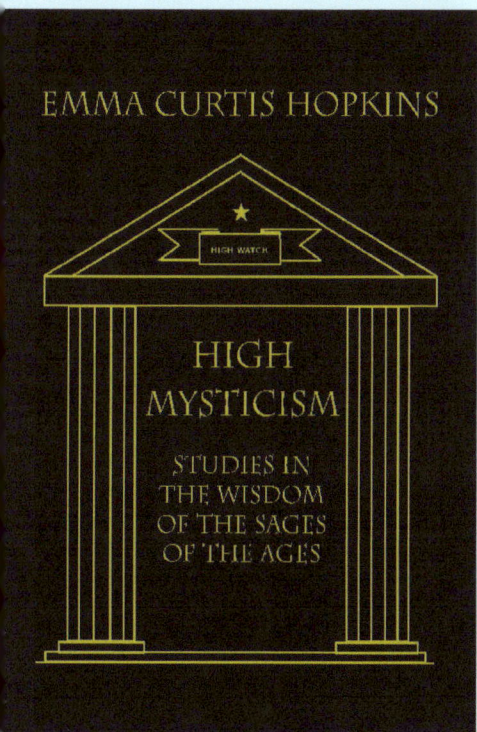

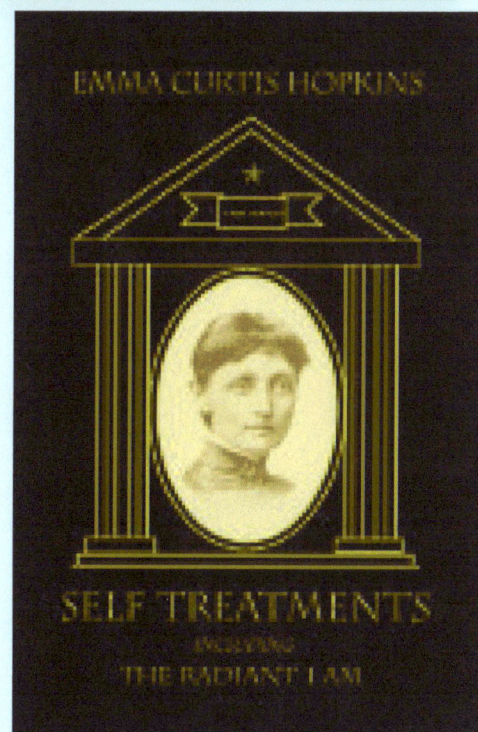

Emma Curtis Hopkins' Class Lessons 1888
The very first of Hopkins' beginning lectures, introducing her version of "Christian Science" as she taught it in her first Seminary from 1886 to 1888.

Emma Curtis Hopkins' Resume: Practice for the twelve lessons in High Mysticism
These practice guidelines were first offered in 1892 to the advanced students and supplement the material in High Mysticism.
Emma Curtis Hopkins' The Gospel Series
Emma Curtis Hopkins shares the "good news" of

unlimited health and prosperity through the power of upward vision and praise—perhaps the most readable of all her lecture series.

Emma Curtis Hopkins' High Mysticism
Studies in the wisdom of the sages of the ages
The culmination of Emma's career, this is her synthesis of the truths to be found in all the world's religions—framed by her 12 lessons.
The original text was printed in 12 little black books in 1920 and has since been reprinted numerous times by numerous printers. This new edition was scanned

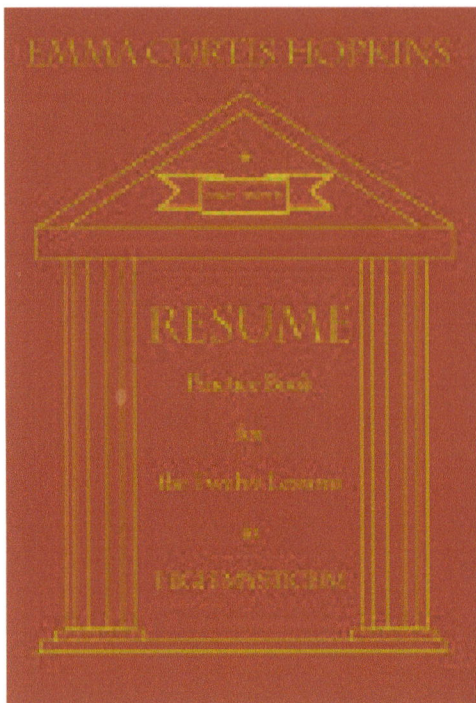

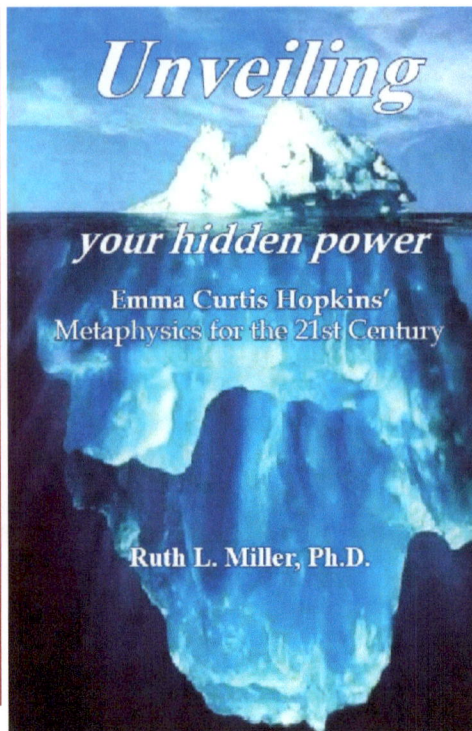

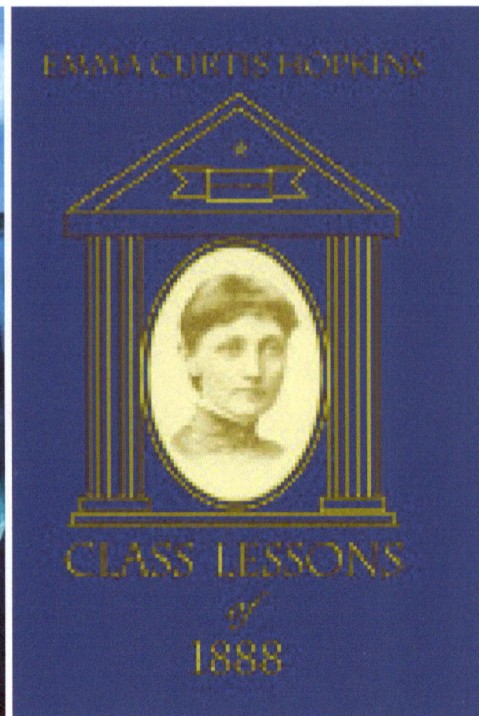

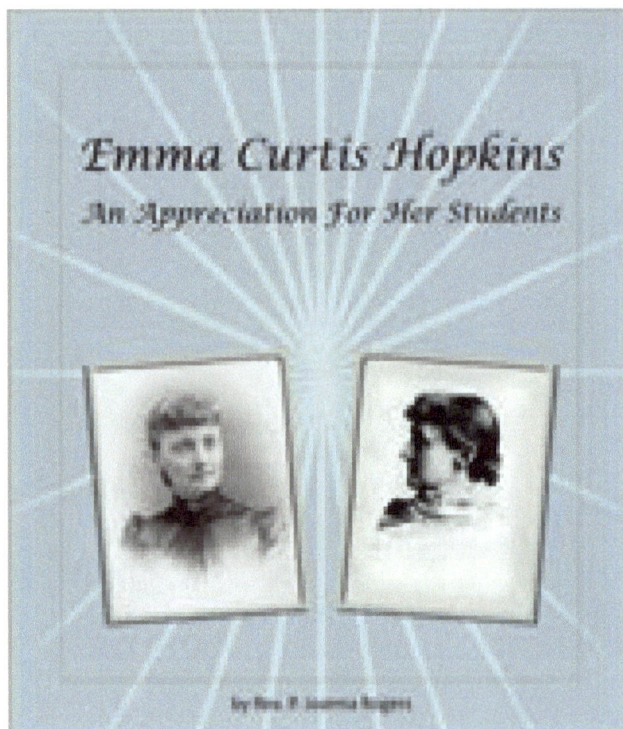

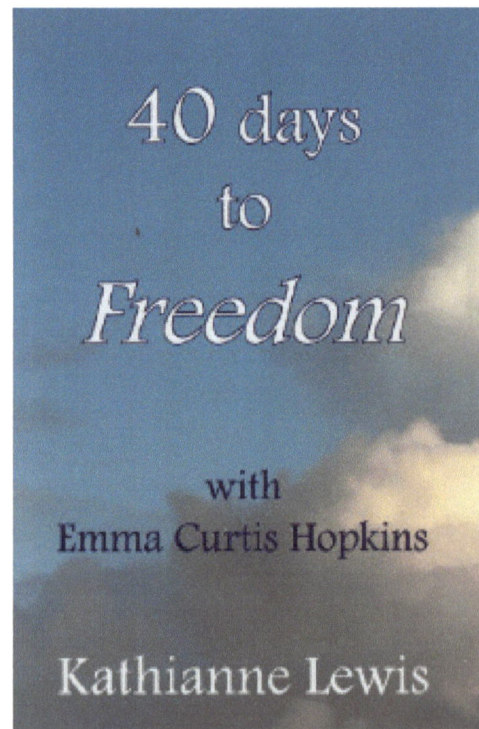

from the original texts and formatted into a single volume with minimal editing.

Emma Curtis Hopkins' Self Treatments, including The Radiant I Am

Taken from her journals and texts, these descriptions of our true nature enliven and inspire the reader, opening the way to new ways of experiencing life.

Emma Curtis Hopkins' Drops of Gold

Gems for each day of the year—one of Emma's earliest publications, now in a daily journal format.

Emma Curtis Hopkins' Judgment Series in Spiritual Science

Another perspective on the 12 Lessons, this time drawing heavily on New Testament scriptures, including John's Revelation.

Emma Curtis Hopkins' Esoteric Philosophy: Deeper Teachings in Spiritual Science

The most difficult to find of all Mrs. Hopkins' works—truly "esoteric," and universal

Healing Drops

What one dwells on the most that he becomes.
We ate good or evil, sick or well, in proportion
as these conditions occupy our thoughts.
                                        -H.P. Smith

"He beholdeth all there is," and, "He beholdeth not iniquity."-Then there is none for him to behold. Blessed reasoning, that lifts us our of pain and sorrow.
-Hopkins.

Matter is never in its right place till it vanishes, leaving only the sweet odors of spirit-Jacques. The profoundest teachings of Oriental philosophy are based on the eternal truth, that all our sense-perceptions are an illusion.
- Evans.

Clasp tightly the little truth you have, and close your ears to the babbling of the crowd.
-Berry.

"I know not where His islands lift
Their fronded palms in air.
I only know I cannot drift
Beyond His love and care."
All the fullness of the possibilities of this creation belong to us when we are in harmony, and it cannot be taken from us. "All things are yours and ye are God's." - N.B. Hughes.

God pities our woes with the love of a Father for his chiled-not by becoming human, and knowing sin, or naught, but by removing our knowledge of what is not. He could not destroy our woes totally if He possessed any knowledge of them. His sympathy is divine, not human
-Eddy.

movers & shakers

Rev. Natalie R. Jean,

a long time Spiritual and Christian Science student and teacher, began her training in 2001 in New York. She studied under the leadership of Reverend Maryse Bastien, founder of Eagle Spirits, a spiritual group dedicated to spiritual teachings. Through Eagle Spirits, Rev. Jean learned the philosophy of many different religions, among them Buddhism, Hinduism, I Am, Mystical, and Esoteric. In 2005, Rev Jean returned to Kensington, Maryland, where she spent her childhood years. Soon thereafter, she was introduced to Reverend Bazemore who created the Church of the Holy Spirit, in Largo MD. After five years of ministerial training with Dr. Bazemore in the field of Christian Science, Rev. Jean became an ordained minister. While under Rev. Bazemore's tutelage, Rev. Jean became fascinated with Christian Science and as a result adopted the teachings of Emma Curtis Hopkins. Over the past four years, this fascination has propelled her to conduct advanced research on Emma's teachings.

Rev. Jean created the ECH Theological Association, Inc. to continue to acquire rare materials on Emma and has dedicated a website in her honor, www.highwatch.net. Currently she is teaching a correspondence course on Emma Curtis Hopkins book entitled "Scientific Christian Mental Practice." She has also republished some of Emma's rare lessons. Recently, Rev. Jean started The ECH Theological Seminary (currently an online school), where she teaches many other lessons taught by Emma Curtis Hopkins. Her students come from around the world, to include Japan, Brazil, California, Denmark, and Chicago.

Rev. Jean has made presentations on Emma's teachings at churches and bookstores in the Maryland area, as well as Florida. Rev. Jean also has an internet radio show on blogtalkradio.com, in which she discusses Emma's lessons as well as her own. She has started to do those lessons in French as well. Her ultimate goal is to open a school where children can start learning these teachings at an early age.

Besides her ministerial training, Rev. Jean received a Bachelor of Arts in Communications at Salisbury State University. She is single and lives in Kensington, MD.

Rev. Doctor Christopher L. Bazemore

Given a vision to enter the ministry at the early age of six, Reverend Doctor Christopher L. Bazemore has deep roots and extensive training in many traditions of Christianity. In the Catholic Church he held local, regional, and national leadership roles. In 1973, Reverend Bazemore was Director of Religious Education at St. Joseph's Parish and St. James Episcopal Church. When the vision came to move to a new aspect of spiritual work in Metaphysical studies, the door opened at the Divine Science Church of the District of Columbia, Georgetown. Reverend Bazemore explored other metaphysical traditions and found many spiritual "foster homes." His first two ordinations were in the Church of the Brotherhood, and the Church of the Holy Spirit (Rose Cross). After intensive study of Religious Science, Science of Mind, and (privately taught) Christian Science, he was ordained through the Divine Science of Brooks Divinity School of Denver, Colorado in February 2002. Over the years, he has participated and presented at numerous Spiritual Conferences across our Nation. In 1978, he presented on Emma Curtis Hopkins, a New Thought teacher from the 1800's who is regarded as the "teachers of teachers." He continues these teachings at the Center of Holistic Living in Largo MD, which he founded in the late 1970s, and where he continues to serve as Pastor with its new name "The Church of the Holy Spirit, United Divine Science." This dedicated community is a source of physical, mental, spiritual and vocational empowerment- a true spiritual resource that blends the highest qualities and experiences of New Thought. Reverend Bazemore is the recently appointed Dean of the United Divine Science Ministerial School.

Reverend Bazemore is also licensed in the State of Maryland and in the District of Columbia as a Psychotherapist, Clinical Professional Counselor, and Certified as a clinical Hypnotherapist. He is considered an expert in the treatment of childhood trauma. Reverend Bazemore earned the Doctorate Degree from California School of Professional Psychology in 2002; a Master's Degree in Counseling from Trinity College and has served as Director of Religious Education and taught in parochial schools. He was granted a Doctorate in Ministry from the Church of the Holy Spirit.

The Reverend has supported and taught courses in metaphysics at Divine Science of Mind, Arlington Metaphysical Chapel, Washington Society of Science of Mind, Church of Two Worlds. The Institute for Spiritual Development, Miracle Light of God, Church of Brotherhood, Astrology Association, Natural Spiritual Science and others. Reverend Bazemore salutes all Light Centers and all students of Truth. He joins them in bringing forth universal consciousness to humankind through the Church of the Holy Spirit and the United Divine Science Ministerial School in Largo.

Reverend Rogers came from England to the United States in 1962. As the wife of a minister, she was very involved with the Unity Church and Sunday School in England, America and Australia for about 14 years. Then, after returning to America, with The United Church of Religious Science, she became a Practitioner.

For Eighteen years she held the position of Electro-Mechanical Designer for the Kitt Peak National Obserbvatory, in Tuscon Arizona. Working there she developed an interest in space and in the universe. This piqued her curiosity into the origins of Religion and Ancient New Thought.

Now, her interests are in the Dead Sea Scrolls and the effects on the beginning of the Christian Church, with a primary interest in Emma Curtis Hopkins and her teachings. She was introduced to Emma Curtis Hopkins about eighteen years ago when she was asked to teach a class comparing her with Ernest Holmes (this course was created by Rev. Ruth Wilkerson of Redlands CA).

Reverend Rogers was ordained by Dr. Lola Mays in Phoenix Arizona in 1986, and soon after founded the Desert Church of the Learning Light in Tucson Arizona. For several years she was the Southern Arizona's District President for the International New Thought Alliance (INTA). Since locating to Ohio she has now taken on the position of District President for Kentucky and Southern Ohio.

In 1998 she presented a program on Hidden Bible Secrets at the INTA Congress in Phoenix Arizona. In 2006 she gave a program on Emma Curtis Hopkins,, and in 2008 participated in the SSMR (Society for the Study of Metaphysical Religion) discussion on Emma Curtis Hopkins.

In 2009, Rev. Rogers published her book Emma Curtis Hopkins: An Appreciation For Her Students, available through www.desert. xpressdesigns.com

Rev. Rogers presented at the 2010 Coloquium, "Allegorical and Mystical Interpretation of the Bible" held at the Universal Truth Center in Miami Gardens FL.

These days Reverend Rogers is spreading her time between Arizona, Colorado, and Ohio enjoying time with her children and grand-children. She devotes most of her time to the Bookshelf, research and writing, but still continues to teach. Alliance (INTA). Since locating to Ohio she has now taken on the position of District President for Kentucky and Southern Ohio.

Michael Terranova has studied most of the major religions of the world. He was one of the first spiritual practitioners at the Abundant Life Center in Vancouver Washington. He holds ministerial degrees from "the "The Teaching of Intuitional Metaphysics" and "The Teaching of the Inner Christ." He has been a minister since 1979. He was Ordained last year by Rev. Marcia Sutton of the "Christ Church of Co-Creation where he has studied the works of Emma Curtis Hopkins for over 15 years. He is a member of WiseWoman Press, which published the works of Emma Curtis Hopkins. His website is www.emmacurtishopkins. com and he also does personal training and consultation about Emma's works.

Hinduism
GANESHA

The elephant-headed god, is easily the most recognizable and lovable of Hindu deities. But pinpointing his various attributes is not quite so simple. He is at once the portly, merry, childlike god and the sage, complex philosopher. He is the presiding deity of material wealth and the lord of spirituality. He removes all impediments for his devotees, but creates all manner of difficulties for the transgressors, men or gods. And associated with every aspect of Ganesha- be it his extraordinary birth, his elephant head, hos broken tusk, his vehicle (the mouse), his appetite or his anger-are scores of myths, each more colourful than the other.

Om. Obeissance to you Ganapati.
Only you are the visible reality.
Only you alone are the creator.
Only you alone are the preserver.
Only you alone are the destroyer.

-Ganesha Athavashirsha Upanishad

The Book of Ganesha by Royina Grewal

Buddhism
DEVELOPING COMPASSION

Before we can generate compassion and love, it is important to have a clear understanding of what we understand compassion and love to be. In simple terms, compassion and love can be defined as positive thoughts and feelings that give rise to such essential things in life as hope, courage, determination, and inner strength. In the Buddhist tradition, compassion and love are seen as two aspects of same thing: Compassion is the wish for another being to be free from suffering; love is wanting them to have happiness. The next matter to be understood is whether it is possible to enhance compassion and love. In other words, is there a means by which these qualities of mind can be increased and anger, hatred, and jealousy reduced? My answer to this is an emphatic, "Yes!" Even if you do not agree with me right now, let yourself be open to the possibility of such development. Let us carry out some experiments together; perhaps we may then find some answers. For a start, it is possible to divide every kind of happiness and suffering into two main categories: mental and physical. Of the two, it is the mind that exerts the greatest influence on most of us. Unless we are either gravely ill or deprived of basic necessities, our physical condition plays a secondary role in life. If the body is content, we virtually ignore it. The mind, however, registers every event, no matter how small. Hence we should devote our most serious efforts to bringing about mental peace rather than physical comfort.

- The Dalai Lama, The Compassionate Life

Kabbalah
THE TREE OF LIFE

The Tree of Life is a symbol of extraordinary richness and meaning. Its roots lie in the ancient mystical lore of Judaism, but it has branched and flowered in many western spiritual traditions. It tells the enchant- ing Story of Life from its far-distant origin to its far- distant future, from its invisible creator to its appointed heir and co-creator, the visible, breathing person. In equal measure everywhere, the same One Spark of Life permeates everything with the same urgency to move, the same impulse to reproduce itself. It is the nature of humanity to perceive, challenge and enjoy this significant oneness. It is likewise the nature of the Tree of Life to unfold this magnificent tale with graphic eloquence and startling surprises. Expect therefore the unexpected. By asserting the duality of all manifesta- tion, the Tree of Life shows how and why every event in the chain of life has two intertwined meanings. One is its individual significance, the other is its relationship to the overall whole. Thereby it uncovers humankind's intimate cosmic link with that supreme life-force with- out definition which words cannot express and whose personified glorious majesty many call God. The Tree of Life will therefore always tell two tales in one single breath: One is the story of humanity in the universe, the other the story of the universe in humanity.

Excerpt from the book, Kabbalah Your Inner Path To Freedom, By Ann Williams-Heller

THE IMPORTANCE OF MINERALS

Often times, people tend to forget about the benefits of minerals, and simply refer to their supplements as vitamins. Yet, vitamins cannot function without the action and interaction of minerals. The body needs the presence of both vitamins and minerals to maintain a proper balance. In order for the body to be in complete balance it requires at least 80 minerals in the correct form. The functions of minerals according to some, are usually limited to building strong teeth and bones. Minerals capabilities are far more valuable. Every living cell requires the presence of minerals for proper function, structure and electrical conductivity.

-Marie Louise Jean

BODY, MIND, SOUL FITNESS

Keeping body, mind, and soul fit is an integral part of our Spirituality. It should be part of our Spiritual practices. We must learn to treat our body as a wonderful temple created by God. We must nourish it with right substance, allowing us to have the greatest amount of energy. As our body is more fit, our mind can be more focused on higher levels of consciousness. We become stable in mind and body. Learn some creative new ways to tone the mind and body.

http://bodymindfitness.com

Fit & Confident

The summer months are the period of the year when women are most self-conscious about their bodies. As temperatures increase, we tend to wear fewer clothes in order to stay cool and comfortable. However wearing fewer clothes forces us to reveal more skin, which often includes areas we may not be completely satisfied with. For most women, our midsection, arms and legs are the top three areas of our bodies that we would like to improve on a fitness level. There is absolutely no dispute that how fit we are affects our self-confidence. When in desired shape, the above mentioned areas help us feel better; which improves professional relationships, friendships and even romantic relationships. It should be noted that we are at our best when we feel good, that is why some women who may not be physically fit, have superb confidence and others who are "skinny" need assurance from others about how they look. Sustainable fitness goes beyond physical aspects. Here are two key points for women to keep in mind as we strive towards being fit and confident in our bodies:

Choose to eat for nourishment

Food serves two purposes for the body; energy and nutrient supply. This means that every time you eat something, your body decides whether it can use the energy from the food to accommodate your lifestyle and or supply all of your organs with the necessary vitamins and minerals they need to function at peak performance. If the food does not serve either purpose, the digested portion is stored as fat and the undigested portion is eliminated. If you lack stamina or muscle tone, practice eating consciously. Read nutrition labels and pay attention to what you are putting in your body.

Stop comparing yourself with other women at the gym

When you compare yourself with other women, you subconsciously diminish your self-confidence. Just like every other living being, all women are uniquely different. One workout regimen cannot work for every woman so you must be open to trying new combinations until you find what works for YOU. Every time I see a woman at a gym with a nice figure, I always compliment her and then ask about her regimen. However, I never try to replicate her workout. Learn to appreciate your body and also show appreciation for other women's bodies.

Physical fitness affects a woman's confidence and like all other aspects of wellbeing, flows within then without. In order to become fit and feel more confident about their bodies, women should eat nutritious foods more often and put more focus on loving their bodies instead of comparing.

– Mankah Angwafo

Prosperity NOW!

My teacher often advised me to "pray until the demonstration." Pray these affirmations continuously and consistently until you receive all the ideas in your heart, mind, body and soul. Pray until you fully experience the desired result: prosperity in all aspects of your life. Know that your words do not return unto you void! You will see results!

(Excerpts from Prosperity Now!)

1. I apply ALL my energies to the accomplishment of my complete, permanent, continuously expanding financial freedom and happiness in every aspect of my life!

12. Divine Love is my Prospering Power!

29. My Financial Success is assured!

31. I praise God for ALL the GOOD that I AM, I have and I AM receiving now!

34. Money is GOOD!

49. There is no limitation, no delay and no obstacle to my millionaire money flow!

126. I was born to be happy, healthy, wealthy and successful in ALL that I do!

Prosperity
NOW!

Daily affirmations
for the completeness
of prosperous living

Prosperity
NOW!

Only GOD

SHAWNA MARIE

Q & A

1.

What does it mean to make no thought of what we shall eat or drink, when Jesus himself fasted forty days, and the wise men of Scripture fasted oft and dieted to suit occasions?

2.

How is the science consistent when in one breath it tell us we can have nothing to ourselves, and in the next breath tells us we can have the desire of our hearts?

3.

When we do not know exactly what course to pursue, how can we be sure it is the true or false self that urges us into doing a certain way?

First –What does it mean to take no thought, etc.? The apparently contradictory nature of word and action here is the divinest harmony to the true scientist. You certainly must not take the least bit of care about what you eat, drink or wear, and yet you are to eat, drink and dress always properly.

Cast all your care-that is, let this Friend so close by you take care on His own shoulders. Go you about healing in His name, teaching the truth as far as you know it; preaching silently or audibly, as judgment dictates, all about the glory and beauty and blessedness of Spiritual Reality.

"Seek ye first the kingdom of God and His righteousness, and all these things shall be added." That is, if you are dealing with spiritual doctrines, the material movements and things will set themselves right. You are not to set the material things and movements right in order to be spiritual, but you are to be spiritual in order to set material things right.

If you are spiritually minded you will often fast many days and not realize it. You do not fast in order to be spiritual, but fast because you are spiritual. Fasting in order to be spiritual, weakens you. It is a taking thought for the body that is forbidden. But fasting that you do when you are already spiritual, strengthens and invigorates you.

You have meat to eat during those hours that the world knows not of. Jesus fasted because he became spiritual as a reward for preaching and teaching Truth. So did the wise men. Then he ate again after the fast. He took no care about it. The Law worked its own way through him and with him.

We must be spiritual by thinking, and telling spiritual Truth. Then we shall find food, raiment and shelter provided and suited to us.
Second –You ask how the science is consistent which tells us we can have nothing, and then says we can have all things? I find that I must scream, vehemently shout, or whisper mysteriously, or whatever way will impress upon you that nothing, nothing, worse than nothing, belongs to

mortality. But all things belong to the spiritual, or truly minded.

Some are hounding me as if I originated the statement of Scripture, that the fulfillment of the desire of the heart belongs by right to every one of us. But I only read of the Law, I do not originate. I did not discover it. Here is the text again which is the key to the whole question: "Seek ye first the kingdom...and all these things shall be added." Renounce the world, the flesh and the devil. That is, deny their reality. Then spiritual powers and spiritual faculties, and spiritual supplies make a new creature. Think what is orderly, true, divine. Speak of these things, teach them; then you will say to the mountains of sorrow, Be gone! And sorrows shall flee away. You shall say to desolation, "I am not desolate," and true companionship will come to you. You shall have more abundantly than you can ask or even think after you have become truly spiritual. Not til then. To the materially-minded nothing is promised. To the spiritually-minded all things are promised.

The desire you have this moment deep down in your heart you ought to have fulfilled. Being your own it ought to come to you.

"Rise the hills,
And swim the sea,
And like thy shadow
Fall on thee."

But it won't come till you are scientific-speak Truth.

It is very strange how our desires change when we become truthful. We set out with denying all the obstacles that keep us from getting our wishes. Barrier after barrier is removed by our denials. Then suddenly we take a new outlook. We would not have the thing we first asked for now. We see things from a more sensible standpoint. We finally get just what we desire. Not what we first asked for, but just what we have come to want. The first desire was a good thing to start off with. The last one to end up with. We shall all be changed."

Third- you ask how to tell the true monition from the false one? Easy enough. Do that which seems just right, or what you seem driven to do and trust your choice. Trust that the Best, the Divine, guided you. Never mind how far away from the Right it seems. Trust that it is Right. Oh! how "you" do like to be trusted! That is, the "you" likes to be trusted by what seems to be you. Trust the Leading. It is the Divine of you. Fear not. Trust. Trust. Trust. Each hour of trusting "yourself" brings you out clearer and clearer as the off-spring of Wisdom. If I were as afraid as so many seem to be, I should be quite swamped because so many condemn me for the bold moves I make. But I jump to a Leading, and let my best beloved cry out against it. Nobody is quite so wise concerning your own matters as yourself. Whatever you do while trying to do the best you can, you have a right to believe in the doing. I know this by experience. I know it by Law. I know it by inspiration.

Peace is granted to the soul who goes to sleep in tune with God.

—Eileen Connolly

The ?!igh LIFE

I threw caution to the wind. Irrepressible desires pulsating within wouldn't let me sleep through the night. One visit to Denver and I was powerfully hooked.

I craved beauty, adventure, excitement and Denver held up a mirror. I see my reflection in this lively, lovely city! Everything about Denver extended an open invitation, offering good times ahead. This invitation was so attractive, so delicious, so personal—I accepted.

COURAGE

Upon further investigation, I discover the distance from West Virginia to Colorado is 20+ hours, 1500+ miles. Am I ready for an adventure of a lifetime? For a good time, I will travel the distance! And, Denver promised refreshingly exciting times.

I took to the road on Memorial Day, beginning my trip on I-64 west. It is my first time traveling in this direction and my anticipation is thirsty for the unknown. The road is open and vehicles are sparse. I planned it that way; hoping my travels would be uninundated. I am challenging an inner fear of traveling on unfamiliar Interstates in unknown directions.

My intuition guides me and I enjoy an eight-hour drive through Kentucky and Indiana to Mount Vernon, Illinois, where I stay the night.

Mount Vernon is a small town in Illinois, where, believe it or not, horse and buggy travel curbside along its roads. Preoccupied with driving, I am unable to capture a snapshot of this replica.

The next morning, I take to the road with the courage and stamina of a pioneer. Within no time, I find myself in St. Louis, Missouri. St. Louis is a happening place! While there, I stop at Gibbol's, a novelty shop that sells costumes: clown/Halloween, make-up, magic and juggling apparatus. I get what I need and get out of town!

St. Louis is full of attractions, distractions and influences, so it's best to know where you're going before you get there or have a destination in mind. Another thing about St. Louis is it can be circuitous. By that, I mean if I don't pay attention to road signs or sign posts, I could end up in a loop of excitement. I'm telling you, St. Louis is full of high times and revelry. Oh, the city has an underground railway. Nice! St. Louis will WOW you! Check out www.explorestlouis.com.

At some point I will revisit St. Louis, but for now, I must get to Denver.

I'm on I-70 west. At this point, I conquer some of my Interstate fears. I mean, what else can I do; out here on major expressways in morning rush hour traffic? The further west I drive, the more engulfed I become in a sea of traffic. Soon, my inner fears abate and turn into excitement. I ride the wave of my adventure!

Speeches have inspired me, movies have moved me, but when I became passionate about this adventure, it fired up my dreams, and life wouldn't allow me to mosey along in a mediocre way. I promised myself, once empowered I would journey through this life fearless, inspiring others to do the same.

Traveling through St. Louis, I somehow avoid wrong turns and manage to get out unscathed.

If you don't know, the mid-west can get blazingly hot. Now you know. When it becomes unbearable, I put up the windows, close the moon-roof and turn on the air conditioner. But most of all, I enjoy driving with open windows, taking in the scent of fresh grass and fragrant flowers in full bloom.

Ahhhhh. Welcome to Kansas! This is the longest leg of my trip. I must drive through the entire state of Kansas!

The expanse of land from left to right driving along I-70 west is peripherally unseeable. The distance is so far and wide. I am awestruck. The beauty of nature in Kansas along I-70 west displays God's awesomeness. Indeed, the land is good and plentiful. Livestock live well here!

WARNING: I gas up my vehicle before venturing into Kansas and gas up whenever I reach half a tank. There are stretches of road along I-70 west in Kansas, where no exits exist for miles. Trust me I did not want to run out of gas anywhere on I-70 west, especially not in Kansas. The land is too vast to traverse by foot. And, traffic, at 75 mph, is few and far between. Besides, I'd be a blur to drivers going 90 in a 75. (Did I mention I had Interstate fears?) They're gone! With wildlife running rampant, I need to be perspicacious driving along I-70 west.

If you can travel the distance of Kansas in a day, then God bless you. I was not doing nonsense! I drove six hours for the day, exited I-70 west at Topeka, Kansas (a thriving, contemporary city), bought my favorite taco bowl, and checked in to a nearby hotel for the evening.

By 6:40 the next morning, I'm in my car. The weather starts out pleasant enough—low 60's. Gradually, the sun rises and stands above Kansas, radiating its powerful summer heat. Herds of livestock—tails dancing in the wind—graze happily inw= grassy meadows.

Kansas is a complex mix of intense heat with high, gusty winds. The wind is so powerful, its impact visibly sways tractor trailers—now that's powerful. So don't try to bypass or overtake these oversized trucks on a curve—it's dangerous.

Driving to the West Coast for the first time, I feel I am creating my own adventure. I know Colorado is mountainous and have no idea if I'll find myself driving along a cliff on a rocky mountain without barriers, but I am up for the challenge. I am driven by the excitement of the unknown. The risk taker within coaxed me way out West and there is no turning back. Like birth, I've reached a point where my only direction was forward.

I am out here like a Bird on A Wire, enjoying my delicious freedom, "like VISA; everywhere I want to be", having an ineffable experience!!! Whenever I want to break free, I never miss an opportunity to experience expansion. Imagination is powerful, but "nothing ever becomes real until it is experienced."

Let me interject something here: Desires are meant to be experienced, dreams are meant to be fulfilled. It's when full potential or self-expression is suppressed, repressed and suffocated that those desires become tortuous yearnings that solidify into regrets—unfulfilled desires that procrastination continuously prevent creating endless inner torment.

I fear regret more than the unknown. And, more than anything, I fear the feeling of regret, which stimulated this adventure. I want to experience all the joy I can stand! I don't want dreams to die inside me unlived. And, I can feel the elation of my Inner Spirit applauding me for allowing It to actively participate, instead of reticently observe.

Driving the expanse of I-70 west, I let the experience unfold on its own, relishing the NOW—realizing that first time experiences are once in a lifetime occurrences, because innovative events can never be experienced again for the first time. Without really keeping track of where I am on my journey (signs and time will do that), I relax and enjoy this moment in time.

Kansas keeps me guessing: What's over that hill? Around that bend? Down that meadow? But the size of wildlife and road kill keeps me car bound. Besides, I am so close to Denver, my hands are glued to the steering wheel. Occasionally, I encounter stretches of road bloody with hoofs, innards and other remnants of wildlife unsuccessful at crossing I-70 west.

Welcome to Colorado! With Denver in close proximity, a surge of thrilling sensations flood through me. I revel in delight and stop to gas up my car. When Interstate lanes expand, you know you're approaching a major city. In Denver, I-70 west expands to eight lanes.

On June 1st, five o'clock rush hour traffic welcomes me to Denver— The Mile High City!

It takes a while, but when traffic permits, I exit I-70 west at 38th & Park Avenue and make my way to downtown Denver. As I round Blake Street, I am immediately introduced to the very prominent Coors Field, surrounded by opulent residential and commercial real estate, local cafés and popular restaurants— The Cheesecake Factory!

The pulse and beauty of downtown Denver is like a flawless diamond—stunningly engaging. By the time I retire for the evening I am tilting from stimulus overload.

Awakened by the warmth of the summer sun, I dress and proceed to live "The High Life." Ω

MUSIC

WYTOLD layers percussive bowing and melodic finger-picking on the cello. Two extra strings on his electric cello allow him to capture the depth and power of a stand-up bass, the rich tonal timbre normally associated the acoustic cello, and the bright crispness of violin solos and harmonies. Wytold records these sounds live on both electric and acoustic cellos to create his own rock-orchestral accompaniment on stage. Wytold recently received a Young Artist Grant from the DC Commission on the Arts and Humanities (DCCAH) to help fund his first solo album: "When Fulvio Finds Celeste". Currently Wytold is actively composing and performing in the Washington, DC area, often accompanied by percussionists Bryan Bowman and Jerry Tolk.

Wytold's composing inspirations come in all shapes, sizes, and colors - literally (he is synesthetic and mentally envisions colors, shapes, and textures that represent melodies, rhythms, and particular cello sounds). Hearing music in his head at almost all waking moments, Wytold often sporadically runs to the cello (or recorder) to figure out and capture a new part or melodic line that he just 'heard' for the first time. Sometimes the rest of the song naturally unfolds in the next five minutes, whereas other songs hibernate for years in various corners of Wytold's consciousness before completion. In any case, Wytold's songwriting always centers on tuning in to what is natural - where it feels like the song should go, and how. The songs are always in motion - building layer upon layer, establishing a foundation for an improvised solo, adding a new harmony to a previously established theme for a different perspective on the same progression, repeating an established chorus to prepare for and emphasize an upcoming change. . . Wytold runs through many possibilities in his head, on his instruments, and by listening to practice recordings until he knows it feels right and fits. **www.wytold.com**

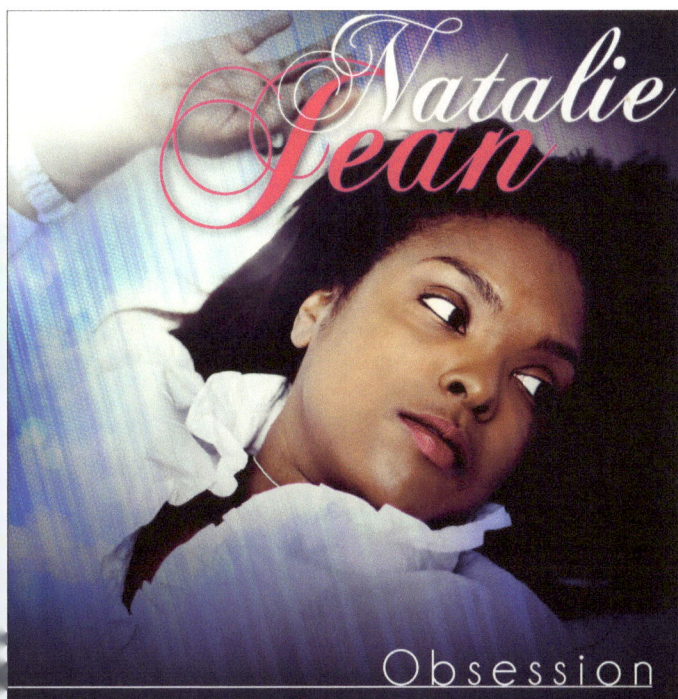

NATALIE JEAN is a talented artist. As a young child she used to sing along with her father, Guy R. Jean, a famous Haitian artist, in their home. Growing up, music was always a passion of hers. She loved to dance and sing. But singing was her greater passion. Natalie Jean started her career by writing poetry. She is an author of a book of spiritual poetry., She then began to write music based on the many experiences that she has had in her life. She is a passionate singer. You can feel every note when she sings. Natalie Jean is mostly influenced by artist such as Lena Horne, Celine Dion, and Etta James. Check out Natalie's hit single "You are my Everything" on her website: **http://www.natalie-jean.com**

practitioners

Rev. Natalie R. Jean

11115 Lund Place
Kensington, MD 20895
240-676-3430
njeanheal@aol.com

*Specializing in all teachings concerning Emma
Curtis Hopkins. We will work together to heal
any situation.I am also available for speaking
engagements, workshops, weddings, baptisms,
unions, and blessings.*

Rita Rogers

1351 Apple Drive
Concord, CA 94518
(925) 680-0967
RMRRSCP@SBCGGLOBAL.COM

Rev. Patrice Julien Behold

10 Avenue de Fontes
34320 Neffies
France
Tel 33. (0) 4.67.38.36.97
info@patricejulien.com

*Rev. Julien also specializes in Self-Identity
through Ho'oponopono, Instuctor and Coordinator
to France, Belgium, Switzerland and French
Speaking territories, and "Chi Breath" Coah
(Japanese Breathing technique), He also officiates,
religious/non religious ceremonies (Wedding,
Baptisms, House Blessing, Land Blessing, etc.)*

Rev. Shawna Marie

Healing Truth Center
PO Box 446
New Rochelle, NY 10802
(914) 813-0906
shawna@healingtruthcenter.com

*Specializes In: Consultations, Speeches, Seminars
& Workshops, Weddings*

Rev. Carole Anderson

Contra Costa Religious Science
1865 Clayton Way
Concord, CA 94519
(925) 825-7553
caroleisspirit@aol.com

classifieds

Reiki

CONSTANT HEALING

Florence Constant, Reiki Practitioner
Bowie, Maryland
(301) 262-8162

Call for an appointment
Available evenings and weekends

The Church of the Holy Spirit

REVEREND DOCTOR CHRISTOPHER BAZEMORE
Dean, United Divine Science Ministerial School
1400 Mercantile Lane, Suite 220
Largo, MD 20774
Phone: 410-685-1440
Fax: 410-332-4141

Individuals seeking education and training as a practitioner and/or minister may contact Rev. Dr. Christopher Bazemore for more information.

Nourish

--a consulting health service-- was created in 2004 for the purpose of providing personalized nutrition and wellness to all—women, men and children. It embraces the notions that "You are what you eat, think and feel", and "your blood type matters." If you consume the foods and supplements that are appropriate for your particular blood type (A, AB, B, O) & have a matching life style, you may be giving yourself the chance to live a longer -healthy life.

Your blood type can determine the foods that are beneficial to you and those that are harmful. In addition, it can reveal your biological strengths and challenges, as well as whether you posses a strong immune system or a sensitive digestive system. Moreover, your blood type is able to signal the foods that can provoke weight gain, depress your immune system and those that can benefit your overall health.

Whatever health challenges you may be facing, Nourish can prepare an individualized health plan that will improve your nutritional deficiencies, balance your hormones, reduce food sensitivities, restore vitality, increase renewal and rejuvenation of cells, enhance organic system's immunity and detoxify the body. The plan can also increase your metabolism for desired weight loss and decrease it to facilitate desired weight gain.

This individualized health plan also includes spiritual and physical oneness through our meditation and exercise programs. These programs will help develop body centeredness, expand your consciousness, enhance self confidence for mental healing and personal and professional improvement, reduce pain and stress and offer weight management techniques.

Nourish also recommends using the ionized alkal-Life or Kangan filtered water system and offers the Bio-Mat Infrared Therapy for further body detoxification.

Nourish's vision is to bring increased awareness that a combination of healthy foods, exercise and spirituality will help us reach the mind, body, spirit-balance that we are all seeking.

For more information please go to *Marie L. Jean website: www. nourishall.com*

EAGLE SPIRITS

An extremely compassionate and caring woman with the divine gifts of healing and prophecy, Christinne Maryse consciously began her spiritual journey at the age of 20. Her mission in life is to guide people to the universal truth of the Light of God within each individual, helping them to find their path here on Earth, and to enable their ascension. For nearly 30 years, it is this very mission to which she has dedicated her life, working closely with Archangel Michael, The Divine Mother Mary, Jesus, Moses, Buddha and many other ascended masters. Living entirely by faith, she is a healer, advisor and teacher to hundreds of individuals across the world, with student groups in NYC, Miami and Haiti.

In addition to her many years of experience in the art of healing and as a psychic analysis, Reike, Dahnak Yoga, hypnotherapy and Yengar Yoga.

She is a fully licensed hypnotherapist with special training in EMDR and is one of the NY Original 100 and U.S.E. 111 members of the International Council of Alternative Research and Education, Reike Sae Chim Master, Yengar Yoga Instructor and a member of the Priesthood of Melchizedek, The Rosicrucians Order Amorc, the free Masons, and the Marteniste.

If you would like to schedule an appointment please email her at eaglespiritsonline@yahoo.com or call her at 301-670-6339.

Christinne Maryse also offers a monthly class that teaches a variety of different religious modalities. From Hinduism, Buddhism, Kabbalah, I AM, etc. This group meets every first Saturday of the month. If interested please contact her.

ECH SEMINARY SCHOOL
CURRENTLY AN ONLINE SCHOOL
www.emmacurtishopkinstheologicalseminary.com

The Emma Curtis Hopkins Theological Seminary is founded to hold daily sessions for the free expression of the extreme conclusions to which Scripture propositions lead.

The Bibles of all times and nations are compared: their miracles are shown to be the results of one order of reasoning, and the absence of miracles shown to be the result of another order of reasoning.

At this Seminary the teachings of inspired writers are proved to be identical with the native inspirations of all minds in common.

We perceive that inherently there is one judgment in all mankind alike. It is restored by the theology taught here. With its restoration we find health, protection, wisdom, strength, prosperity.

"At the same time my reason returned unto me, and for the glory of kingdom, mine honor and brightness returned unto me." Dan. iv. 36.

Theological Premise In Mental Science

The Divine Being, clothed in omnipresence, omnipotence, omniscience, is the unfailing life, health, strength, support, defense and inspiration of the universe. The opposite of Divine Being has no being existence.

Under the touch of inspiration for manifesting the world and all things therein:

Mind is the ruling principle.
Mind is as great and free as it has courage to eliminate ideas.
Mind is as powerful, wise, capable as it has courage to say I AM.
Mind is able to demonstrate, embody, substantiate as much as it had boldness to command.
Mind is soul, spirit, or neither; mortal or immortal, heaven, or hell, according to its own decree or "let it be done."
Mind senses and experiences all that it names.
Mind reads the book of its own life, history and prophecy, in all that it senses.
Mind illuminates by one line of reasoning and darkens by another.
The mental notice cannot be hidden.
Mind lives by and on its own faith.
Mind as the ruling principle has as good judgment as its will and meekness do agree.
Mind is self-increasing, self-strengthening, self-informing.
Its understanding is its Divine Self, or Divine Being, which needeth not that any man should teach it.

"I consulted with myself."
Neh. 5:7

EMMA CURTIS HOPKINS THEOLOGICAL ASSOCIATION, INC.

The Emma Curtis Hopkins Theological Association, Inc., was formed for the purpose of acquiring more of Emma's teachings for the purpose of republishing, promoting, and teaching. The Association was formed by me, Rev. Natalie R. Jean in 2007. Now, I think it is time to engage the devoted Emma students to come and join the association. You can join as a member or you can get elected to the board. If you are on the board you will be required to pay a fee and minimal monthly dues. You will also have to participate in monthly meetings via Skype. If you opt to become a member you will have a yearly fee. It is time that we engage the world in the wonderful and powerful teachings of Emma Curtis Hopkins.
Member Yearly Fee $30

Board Member Fee $50 and monthly due $5

As a member of ECH Theological Association, Inc, you will enjoy many benefits, which include:

- Membership Card
- Discounts on books and events
- Access to a valuable library of books, tapes and videos
- Information on new teachings bible lessons
- Contribution to the only magazine (which will be coming in the near future)
- Participation in all member meetings.
- Discount on courses being offered at the online Seminary

As a Board Member:

- You will enjoy the same benefits as a member, but they will also include:
- Collaborating on the Emma Movement, by giving ideas on how teachings can be brought out into the world
- Participating monthly meeting
- Gifting of Business Cards

Please fill out the application form if you are interested for either position. If you are interested in becoming a Board member, I will contact you with further details. Fill out the form on www.highwatch.net

HEALING TRUTH CENTER

Healing Truth Center is a multimedia ministry and resource for inspiration, education and healing. Founded by CEO and Spiritual Leader Shawna Marie, Healing Truth Center provides products, consultations, speeches, seminars and workshops that empower souls worldwide in their personal process of spiritual discovery and healing.

"There is a Presence and a Power greater than us. As we grow in our understanding of this Presence... As we tap into this Power... we transform ourselves and the world for the greater good of all."
~Shawna Marie

Beliefs:
There is Only God - One Presence, One Power, One Knowledge that is ALL Good, in ALL, as ALL, for ALL, and through ALL, at ALL times.
Healing is the result of an expanded awareness of God as "Good" and the Healing Power of Holy Spirit cultivated through prayer, meditation, spiritual study, and joyful spiritual living.

Everyone can be happy, healthy, prosperous, satisfied and successful in ALL areas of life: health, career, relationships, money supply and spirituality.

Products:
Prosperity NOW! Affirmation of the Day, Book and Prayer Movement

Living in Spiritual Perspective Radio, TV & Blog

Services:
Consultations
Speeches, Seminars & Workshops
Weddings

Web Links:
Blog - ShawnaMarieAC.com
TV - HealingTruthCenter.com/tv
Radio - HealingTruthCenter.com/radio

Facebook - facebook.com/shawnamarieac

Twitter - twitter.com/shawnamarieac

Youtube - youtube.com/shawnamarieac

Healing Truth Center is especially grateful to our Advisory Committee: Rev. Dr. Christopher Bazemore, Chey Blake, Michelle Christie, Norma Dwyer, Rev. Alicia Hill, Gina Jackson, Mari Torres-Lee and Rev. Dr. Robert Yarbrough

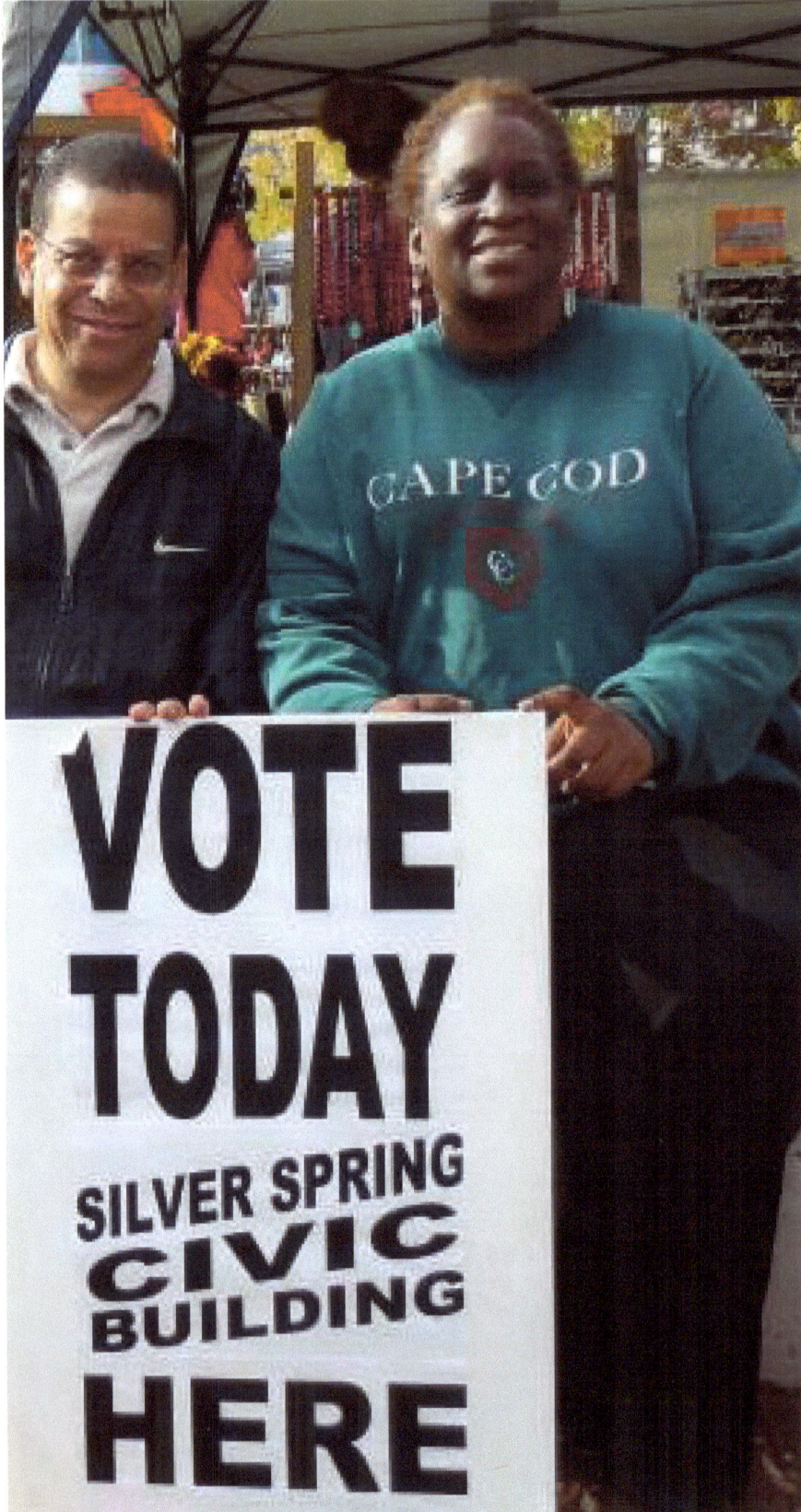

In memorium

Karla Walker

How could this be
I still hear your voice
Echoing these walls
A Beautiful Sister
A Soul like no other
Plans were made
Justice would prevail
A fighter to the very end
I say "Gone too soon"
God had another plan
Your wings were made
Now you soar in the heavens
Watching over the land
While holding God's Hand

Best Friend

When our eyes met
I knew you would be the one
I will never forget
How your energy pierced my soul
Making me whole
You belonged to me
And I to you
You were my great best friend
One that I will remember to the very end
You were sent from above
To teach me how to love
Some will not comprehend
Or even understand
They may not see
The bond between you and me
You are the greatest part of who I Am
Soul to Soul
Heart to heart
I give thanks for your unconditional love
Strong till the very end
I know that we will meet again

-Natalie Jean

Infinitus Amou

www.ingramcontent.com/pod-product-compliance
Lightning Source LLC
Chambersburg PA
CBHW042014080426

42735CB00002B/52